CW01506755

B1 Preliminary for Schools

Trainer

Six Practice Tests without answers

Second edition

1

Cambridge University Press
www.cambridge.org/elt

Cambridge Assessment English
www.cambridgeenglish.org

Information on this title: www.cambridge.org/9781108528870

© Cambridge University Press and UCLES 2019

First published 2019

20 19 18 17 16 15 14 13 12 11 10 9 8 7 6 5 4 3 2 1

Printed in Malaysia by Vivar Printing

A catalogue record for this publication is available from the British Library

ISBN 978-1-108-52887-0 Student's Book without answers with audio
ISBN 978-1-108-52888-7 Student's Book with answers with audio

The publishers have no responsibility for the persistence or accuracy
of URLs for external or third-party internet websites referred to in this publication,
and do not guarantee that any content on such websites is, or will remain,
accurate or appropriate. Information regarding prices, travel timetables, and other
factual information given in this work is correct at the time of first printing but
the publishers do not guarantee the accuracy of such information thereafter.

Contents

Introduction

Who is this book for?

If you are aged between 11 and 15 and want to take **B1 Preliminary for Schools**, this book is for you!

Why is this book called 'Trainer'?

This book is called '**Trainer**' because it is full of exercises to help you get better and better at doing each part of **B1 Preliminary for Schools**. So, complete all the exercises, then do all the practice papers. If you train and work hard, you will soon be ready to take **B1 Preliminary for Schools**!

How do I use this book?

First do the exercises on each **Training** page. Then do the task on the **Exam Practice** page and check your answers.

Tests 1–2: Training

On Training pages (Tests 1 and 2 only), you will find:

 Cambridge Learner Corpus

This shows information about mistakes that some **B1 Preliminary for Schools** candidates make. If you do these useful exercises, you will learn <u>not</u> to make these mistakes when <u>you</u> do the exam.

This provides ideas to help you do well in the exam. For example: *If you find it difficult to talk about one of the pictures, quickly move onto another picture.*

Remember

This gives a quick reminder about grammar points or vocabulary that you should learn. For example: *We can say* allow someone <u>to</u> do something *or* let someone do something *(without* to*).*

Tests 1–2: Exam Practice

On Exam Practice pages in Tests 1 and 2, you will find:

- a **B1 Preliminary for Schools** exam task for you to try and complete
- further tips and advice to help you with different parts of the task.

Tests 3, 4, 5 and 6

When you finish Tests 1 and 2 you will be ready to do some complete **B1 Preliminary for Schools** Practice Tests.

Tests 3, 4, 5 and 6 are just like real **B1 Preliminary for Schools** Reading, Writing, Listening and Speaking papers. Doing these tests will give you extra help to prepare for the exam.

Keep a record of your scores as you do the tests. You may find that your scores are good in some parts of the test, but you may need to practise other parts more. Make simple tables like this to record your scores:

Reading	Part 1	Part 2	Part 3	Part 4	Part 5	Part 6
Test 3						
Test 4						
Test 5						
Test 6						

Other features of the *B1 Preliminary for Schools* Trainer

- **Visual material**

In the Speaking test the examiner will give you a booklet with photographs and pictures in it. The visual material in the colour section from pages C1–C16 will help you practise and become familiar with the type of pictures and photographs you will see in the test and help you increase your confidence.

- **Sample Answer Sheets**

Look at these to see what the *B1 Preliminary for Schools* answer sheets in the test look like and learn how to complete them. Ask your teacher to photocopy them so that you can use them when you do your practice tests.

- **Downloadable audio online**

Listen to these to practise the Listening paper. You will also need to listen to these to complete some of the Training exercises and to hear a demonstration of each part of the Speaking test.

The structure of the *B1 Preliminary for Schools* exam

The *B1 Preliminary for Schools* exam has four papers:

Reading: 45 minutes

There are six parts to the Reading test and you will need to be able to read and understand a range of texts from short notices and messages to longer articles from brochures, magazines and newspapers. For two of the parts you will also have to choose the correct words to complete a text – in one, you choose from the words provided and in the other you use your own words.

Writing: 45 minutes

In the two parts of the Writing test you will write an email and an article or a story, each about 100 words long.

Listening: 30 minutes (approximately)

In the four parts of the Listening paper you will need to be able to listen and understand people who are talking together and people who are giving information about something. You will have to choose or write the answers to the questions which are about what these people say. Don't worry! The people talk about everyday topics, speak clearly and don't talk fast.

Speaking: 12 minutes (pairs) 17 minutes (groups of three)

You will need to be able to listen and understand what the examiner is saying. You will have to answer some questions about yourself, and you will need to speak on your own about a photograph. You will then be given some pictures to look at and you will use the pictures to do a speaking task with another candidate. In the final part you and the other candidate will answer questions based on the topic in the pictures. Usually candidates take the Speaking test with just one other candidate, but sometimes they do it in groups of three. For this reason there are additional pictures for Candidate C in this book.

Frequently asked questions

Is my English good enough for B1 Preliminary for Schools?

The level of the exam is Council of Europe Level B1. At B1 level, students can:

- understand the main points of straightforward instructions or public announcements
- understand instructions in classes and on homework given by a teacher
- understand factual articles in magazines and letters from friends expressing personal opinions
- understand most information of a factual nature in their school subjects
- ask simple questions and take part in factual conversations in school
- talk about things such as films and music and describe their reactions to them
- write letters or make notes on familiar or predictable matters
- take basic notes in a lesson
- write a description of an event, for example a school trip.

Note that different students have different strengths and weaknesses. Some may be good at speaking but not so good at writing; others may be good at reading but not so good at listening. The B1 level 'Can Do' statements above simply help teachers understand what *B1 Preliminary for Schools* candidates should generally be able to do at this level.

What grade do I need to pass B1 Preliminary for Schools?

There are two passing grades for *B1 Preliminary for Schools*: Pass with Merit and Pass. Candidates who don't get a passing grade but show that they have ability in English at a slightly lower level (Council of Europe Level A2) get level A2 on their certificate. Candidates who score below level A2 get a fail grade.

Basic user		Independent user		Proficient user	
A1	**A2**	**B1**	**B2**	**C1**	**C2**
	A2 Key for Schools	B1 Preliminary for Schools	B2 First for Schools		

What marks do I need to pass each paper, and to pass the exam?

Candidates do not have to get a certain mark to pass each paper in the exam. The final mark for **B1 Preliminary for Schools** is the total number of marks from all four papers: Reading, Writing, Listening and Speaking. There are an equal number of possible marks for each paper in **B1 Preliminary for Schools**.

How can I find out about my performance in each paper of B1 Preliminary for Schools?

Before you get a certificate you will get a Statement of Results telling you how well you did in **B1 Preliminary for Schools**. As well as your result and your score out of 100, it also gives you your 'Candidate Profile'. This is an easy-to-read graph that shows how you performed in all the papers of the exam compared to all the other candidates taking the same exam. If you do not get the score that you wanted, the Candidate Profile will show you which of the skills (reading, writing, listening and speaking) you did well in and which you need to improve.

Is B1 Preliminary for Schools suitable for candidates of any age?

B1 Preliminary for Schools is more suitable for students who are at school and aged from 11–15. To make sure that the material is interesting for this age group and not too difficult or too easy for the B1 level, all the parts of the Reading, Writing, Listening and Speaking papers are pre-tested. This means that different groups of students try the materials for each part of the tests first. The material will then only be used in real exams if the results of the pre-tests show that they are suitable for candidates who want to take **B1 Preliminary for Schools**.

Can I use pens and pencils in the exam?

In **B1 Preliminary for Schools** candidates must use **pencil** in the Reading and Listening papers. It's useful for you if you want to change one of your answers on the answer sheet. However, you must use a **pen** for the Writing paper.

What happens if I don't have enough time to finish writing?

You can only be given marks for what you write on the answer sheet, so if you do not complete this then you will miss the chance to show the examiner what you can do and how good your English is. Watch the clock and plan your time carefully. Do not waste time writing your answers on other pieces of paper in Reading and Writing; however, in the Listening test it is a good idea to write your answers on the question paper first. You will have time at the end to move your answers from the question paper to your answer sheet.

If I write in capital letters, will it affect my mark?

No. You do not lose marks for writing in capital letters in **B1 Preliminary for Schools**. Whether you choose to use capital letters or not, you should always make sure that your handwriting is clear and easy to read. Remember that the examiners can't mark a piece of writing that they can't read!

In this part you:

- **read** five different short texts, e.g. signs, notices, emails, messages, advertisements

- **choose** which option (A, B or C) means the same as the short text

TIP Decide what kind of text each is, e.g. a label, and where you might see it.

FOCUS: TEXT TYPES AND FUNCTIONS

1 Look at the five short texts. Match **1–5** with these text types:

advertisement   label on packet   notice in school
road sign   sign in park

① School café opening hours:
10.30–11.00
12.30–13.30
14.30–15.00

② Parking not permitted within 25 metres of school entrance

③ Take three times a day after meals. Tablets must not be given to children under 12.

④
DANGER
Thin ice on lake during winter months

⑤ **FOR SALE**
Ski boots size 38
Excellent condition
Make me an offer!

2 Look again at **1–5**. What is the purpose of each text? How do you know?

- **a** to warn of danger
- **b** to give information
- **c** to try to sell something
- **d** to say what you must not do
- **e** to say what you must and must not do

3 Choose the correct words.

1 We *mustn't / don't need to* talk when we are doing science exams.

2 At our school we *mustn't / don't have to* wear a uniform.

3 You *don't need to / mustn't* come with us if you don't want to.

4 If you're tired, I think you *need to / have to* have a break.

GRAMMAR: *MUST | HAVE TO | NEED TO*

👁 *B1 Preliminary* candidates often make mistakes with the modal verbs *must, have to* and *need to* and their negative forms.

4 **Complete the sentences with *must, have to, mustn't* or *don't have to*.**

1 Do you .... get up early every morning?

2 Pupils .... make a noise outside the exam room.

3 We .... go to school during the holidays.

4 You .... always be polite to your teachers.

5 I live near my school, so I .... walk far in the morning.

6 In football you .... touch the ball with your hands, unless you're the goalkeeper.

Remember

You don't have to means that it is not necessary (but you can if you want to). *You mustn't* means *Don't do it!*

FOCUS: THE WRITER'S PURPOSE

5 **Look at texts 1–4 below. For each one, decide:**

- what kind of text type it is
- who is sending the message/email
- who receives the message/email
- why they are writing

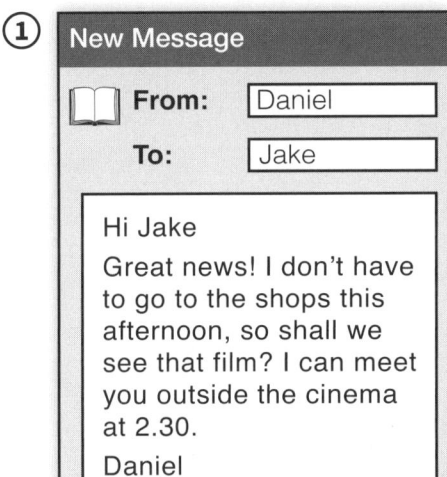

① **New Message**

From: Daniel

To: Jake

Hi Jake
Great news! I don't have to go to the shops this afternoon, so shall we see that film? I can meet you outside the cinema at 2.30.
Daniel

② Hi Rose
Thanks for reminding me it's Isaac's birthday next week. I mustn't forget to send him a card.
Francesca

TIP For messages, emails and notes, think about who the writer and reader might be.

③ Hi Lewis,
I can drive you to your friend's house when I get home this evening, but you must finish your homework before we go out.
Mum

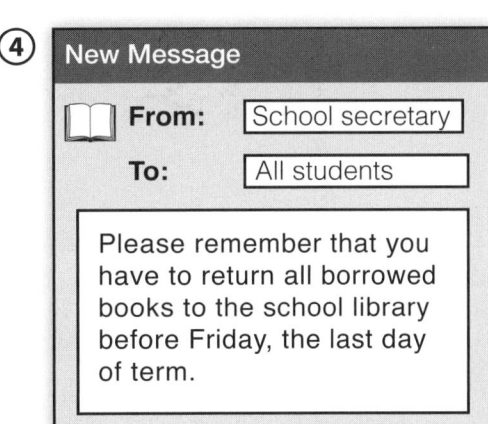

④ **New Message**

From: School secretary

To: All students

Please remember that you have to return all borrowed books to the school library before Friday, the last day of term.

Questions 1–5

For each question, choose the correct answer.

1

Anton,
When you see your sister at the basketball match later, can you make sure she remembers that Dad's coming to fetch her instead of me? I've tried ringing, but her phone's off.
Thanks,
Mum

A Anton has to check his sister knows about the arrangements for getting home.

B Anton should remind his sister to switch her phone back on.

C Anton needs to ask his sister if she's taking part in a sports event later.

2

From the famous novel by
Ben Whitham:
a film about a bear's adventures.
Fun for all the family!"

This film is

A about a family of wild animals.

B not suitable for people under a certain age.

C based on a popular fiction book.

3

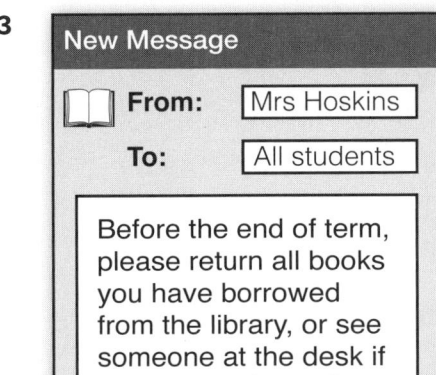

New Message

From: Mrs Hoskins

To: All students

Before the end of term, please return all books you have borrowed from the library, or see someone at the desk if you want to have them for the summer holiday.

A You must take back all the library books you've got before the summer holiday.

B If there are library books you want, borrow them before the end of term.

C To keep any library books for holiday reading, ask staff at the desk.

4

Tina,
When you come round tonight, can you bring that earring you found outside school the other day? I think I know who it belongs to, so I'll return it.
Thanks,
Nicola

A Nicola is telling Tina to return something she was lent recently.

B Nicola is hoping she can give a lost item back to its owner.

C Nicola is asking for help to find a lost earring belonging to her.

5

BIKES FOR HIRE

Adult cycles always available

Children's cycles – book in advance

8 a.m. – 9 p.m.

Only €20 per day

A Families may not find suitable bikes for everyone unless they've reserved them.

B You can always find a range of bikes for hire here.

C Bikes aren't available for customers' use in the evenings.

In this part you:

- **read** five descriptions of people and eight short texts on a variety of subjects
- **match** what each person requires with information in one of the eight texts

FOCUS: PARAPHRASING

1 Match the expressions about people with the expressions about apartments.

Information about people looking for apartments	Information about apartments
always uses public transport	extremely low prices
cannot afford to spend much	has its own gym
dislikes noise	is in a quiet neighbourhood
is very sociable	next to a leisure centre open every evening
likes to keep fit	bus stop nearby
works until 5.30 p.m.	opportunities to meet new people

FOCUS: IDENTIFYING KEY WORDS

2 Read this description of someone who wants to go away on holiday. Underline the words and phrases that tell you exactly what she wants.

Hannah wants to go to a really lively place where everything stays open late. It should also offer some top-class cultural attractions and high-quality accommodation.

FOCUS: MATCHING KEY WORDS WITH PARAPHRASES

3 Read these descriptions of three holidays and decide which of A–C would be the most suitable for Hannah.

A Study tours

Travel to a country famous for its culture and visit cities of historical interest, attending lessons and meeting local experts. To keep costs down you stay in inexpensive hostels. Favourite destinations include Italy for art and Austria for classical music.

B Sunshine destinations

This seaside holiday includes your flights abroad, transport to the (rather basic) hotel, evening entertainment and meals. There's not much to do in the local town, but if you enjoy relaxing on a beautiful beach, it's perfect!

C City breaks

Stay in a luxury hotel in one of the world's most exciting cities: New York. Enjoy the world-famous Museum of Modern Art and the theatres of Broadway. Then, by night, have fun in the city that never sleeps!

4 In pairs, underline the expressions in the correct text (A, B or C) that have similar meanings to the words and phrases you underlined in Exercise 2.

Questions 6–10

For each question, choose the correct answer.

TIP Underline the key words for each person. Then read the eight texts quickly to find the information that matches. Remember this is often expressed in different words.

The young people below all want to find an art course to attend.
On the next page there are descriptions of eight art courses.
Decide which art course would be the most suitable for the people below.

6
Rafa wants to produce artwork to support his art college application. He's written stories, which he'd like to publish, and wants to learn how to include drawings in them, without using a computer.

7
Simona enjoys creating art on her computer, and wants to find ways to improve the posters she makes on it. She also wants to share what she's done with other students on the course.

8
Andrei wants to try different painting techniques, and have trips to see the work of famous painters, to get ideas for his own pictures. He'd also like to try painting outdoors.

9
Nicola enjoys printing by hand. She wants to print the patterns she's created onto different materials, for her mother to make into clothes, and also learn basic printing techniques to use at home.

10
Karl enjoys taking photos of his family, and wants to use them as a basis for the art he produces. He'd like to go somewhere that also offers private lessons.

Art Courses

A   Get Artistic

Teachers here always have ideas to get you drawing, painting and printing – but you can use your own material, too. The studio-based course focuses on portraits – you'll learn how to develop whatever you've brought, or use famous portraits, to create pictures of people. One-to-one sessions also available.

B   Art Attack!

Learn how to create pictures, perhaps based on your own writing, to put into a short book or poster, using simple techniques that don't require technology. Discover, too, how to put a book together, with a professional-looking cover designed and hand-printed by you. Perfect for anyone considering further studies in art.

C   Art and imagination

If you like designing clothes, you'll enjoy learning to use special computer software here to create and print out designs for tops, shoes and hats that people would love to wear! You'll go home with a folder of work, perfect to present when applying for a higher-level art course. Individual classes also available.

D   Create!

Draw and paint in different situations – in the studio or even in the park! Gallery visits are also included, and you're taught how to base your work on studies of landscapes and portraits by well-known artists. Teachers also encourage you to experiment with various styles and methods.

E   More Art Now!

Improve how you paint people and places on this studio-based course. The teachers bring in work, ranging from photos to posters, to give you ideas. And use the studio website to show your work and exchange ideas with other students – useful for anyone wishing to study art at a higher level.

F   Art Workshop

Do some drawings, in the studio or outside, or bring along your own. The teachers will then help you to turn them into wonderful printed designs, using simple methods you can try yourself after the course. You'll then transfer your designs onto cotton and silk, using special paints – perfect to use in sewing projects afterwards.

G   Do it yourself

Try making art to go with your stories here – working inside or outside! You'll get ideas from books showing famous paintings and cartoons, and then create and print pictures of people to accompany your stories, using digital design techniques. There's even one-to-one teaching if you'd prefer.

H   The Studio

Come and experiment with digital design. You'll get great ideas through research, then using special software, create your pictures and add details on screen, whether it's clothes, people, books or something to put on the wall. Upload your work on the studio website and get opinions from your classmates there – and comment on theirs!

In this part you:

- **read**   a long text that includes opinions and feelings
- **choose**   a correct answer (A, B, C or D) from five multiple-choice questions

GRAMMAR: REPORTING VERBS

1   Complete the sentences with the correct form of these verbs.

| apologise | blame | explain | invite | offer |
| promise | recommend | warn | | |

1   The water was very deep, so Jessica .... him not to jump into it.
2   I .... that you buy one of these hair dryers. I've got one myself and it's great!
3   Max .... to me for damaging my bike when he borrowed it.
4   The boys .... that they would be late because they had an exam after school.
5   The shop .... to fix my phone by Tuesday, but it still wasn't ready by Friday.
6   Amelie .... me to her birthday party, which was really kind of her.
7   My cousin Miguel .... to give me a lift into town in his new car.
8   My mum .... me for the mess in the kitchen, but really it was my sister's fault.

B1 Preliminary candidates often make mistakes with reporting verbs.

2   Correct the grammar error in each sentence, without changing the verb given.

1   My friend <u>suggested to go</u> to the park to play football.
2   Zara <u>explained the teacher</u> that she had been off school because of illness.
3   We <u>recommend you to wash</u> this item of clothing in warm water.
4   The thief <u>refused saying</u> where he had hidden the stolen diamonds.
5   My dad <u>reminded me I check</u> the tyres on my bike before I went out.
6   Aisha <u>offered helping me</u> with my maths homework.
7   Our literature teacher <u>encouraged we read</u> more books at home.
8   I tried to <u>persuade my parents letting me</u> stay out late, but they said 'no'.

FOCUS: UNDERSTANDING PURPOSE IN EXAM QUESTIONS

3   Look again at the corrected sentences in Exercise 2. What is the subject's purpose in each of (1–8)?

Example   1 to make a suggestion.

FOCUS: UNDERSTANDING GIST

4 Quickly read this paragraph below and answer the questions.

The four of us came down the mountain later than we had intended, but it had been well worth spending some time there, admiring the fantastic views from the peak. The track that led to the village far below was steep and icy, but it was the only way down and we had to get there before dark. Then suddenly it started to snow, and it became more difficult to follow the path. I hadn't mentioned our plans to local people before we set out that morning, but when I realised my phone didn't work up there I suddenly wished I had, just in case.

1 What kind of text is it from?
   a an advertisement
   b a travel guide
   c a story
2 What was the speaker doing?
   a relaxing in a village
   b climbing down a mountain
   c watching some people climbing
3 How did she feel?
   a a little worried
   b rather bored
   c angry with the other people
4 What is the speaker's main purpose in the paragraph?
   a to blame other people for her situation
   b to admit she had made a mistake
   c to encourage others to do the same climb

FOCUS: UNDERSTANDING MULTIPLE-CHOICE QUESTIONS

5 Look at the multiple-choice question below about the paragraph in Exercise 4. Answer questions 1–3.
   1 What reporting verb does it use?
   2 Where should you look in the paragraph for the answer?
   3 Which is the best answer, A, B, C or D?

When the snow began to fall, the speaker regretted
   A leaving her mobile phone in the local village.
   B going climbing without telling anyone else.
   C spending so long at the top of the mountain.
   D taking that route down towards the village.

6 Work in pairs. Match the incorrect answers (A, B, C or D) with the parts of the text that show they are wrong.

Questions 11–15

For each question, choose the correct answer.

Our Great Ocean Road adventure

by Donna Waverley

My family and I recently went to Australia, to see my grandparents. But before we visited them, we went sightseeing along the Great Ocean Road, on the Australian coast.

Dad had intended to drive, but even though he was used to driving miles without getting exhausted, he then read on the website that the road wouldn't be an easy drive, with a number of sharp bends. Anyway, we thought he deserved to enjoy the fantastic views too, which he couldn't do as our driver. So instead, we persuaded him to book discount bus tickets and off we went.

Our first stop was where wild kangaroos lived – and Dad and I were taking a walk when a big one appeared! For a moment, it seemed to consider coming towards us, which made me slightly nervous – but then it went off along the road, stopping to check if we were following. Although it was with us a while, I was so excited I didn't even manage to pull out my camera. Then it looked back once more, and went off into the bushes.

That wasn't the only wildlife we saw. I thought it unlikely we'd see Australia's famous koala bears during our short visit, as I'd heard they were rare – but we weren't disappointed at our next stop. In fact, we discovered there were roughly six million in that area! Sadly, some gum trees they were in had very few leaves left, which people told us was because of the koalas, although I'd read that lack of water is actually the problem. Still, I guess they looked cute, and were easy to find – we just followed the tourists looking up into the trees!

Dad had booked a campsite for the night, with ready-made tents – for an adventure! I wasn't sure about that, but they were actually luxury tents, within walking distance of some famous rocks and other places we hoped to visit. However, Dad also said the sounds of wild creatures would help us sleep. That sounded worrying – until the 'wild creatures' turned out to be frogs! So I was embarrassed by my fears – and kept awake by the frogs! But we had fun making meals together – we'd brought food, as we knew there'd be nowhere to eat.

In fact, this whole trip was fantastic!

11 Donna's Dad decided not to drive the Great Ocean Road himself because

    A he realised he wouldn't enjoy the views as much.

    B he thought it would be too tiring for him.

    C he discovered the bus would be a cheaper option.

    D he found out the route was very challenging.

 TIP Remember that most questions are about attitude and opinions, not facts.

12 When Donna saw a kangaroo along the route, she was

    A worried that it might approach her.

    B amazed at the size of it.

    C sad that it didn't stay with them long.

    D disappointed that she had forgotten her camera.

13 Donna says that the koala bears they saw were

    A responsible for damage to the trees.

    B even more attractive than people had told her.

    C more common than she'd expected.

    D very skilled at hiding away from tourists.

14 What was Donna's opinion of the place where they stayed?

    A She found it was less comfortable than she'd hoped.

    B She liked the fact that it was convenient for sightseeing.

    C She enjoyed hearing the sounds of nature as she slept.

    D She was disappointed there was no restaurant nearby.

15 What might Donna write in her blog during the trip?

A

> The bus we're travelling on is pretty comfortable, with great views from the window. Grandma and Grandad are enjoying it, too!

B

> We can see quite a lot as we drive along. I just wish we could stop and get out to explore properly.

C

> Yesterday we went to see some huge rocks near our campsite – and we were really impressed! I'm surprised they're not well known.

D

> I wasn't looking forward to camping, in case there were wild animals, but we haven't seen anything at all dangerous, so I feel silly now!

In this part you:

- **read**   a text from which five sentences have been removed
- **choose**   from a list of eight sentences to replace the missing sentences

GRAMMAR: REFERENCE WORDS

👁   *B1 Preliminary* candidates often make mistakes with reference words.

1   **Choose the correct words in these sentences.**

     1   Two young children asked me where classroom 32 was, so I walked there with *those / them*.

     2   When I saw Grace at the party, I thanked her for her letter, *it / which* had arrived the day before.

     3   Nobody else saw the car stop outside the house, but Emily *saw / did*.

     4   Somebody phoned the police. *It / They* arrived in ten minutes and arrested the man.

     5   We decided to turn left at the crossroads. *These / This*, we soon found out, was a bad decision.

     6   There were two bikes for sale in the shop. Liam bought the newer *one / ones*.

     7   Going by bus sounds like a good idea. *It / They* would be cheaper than the train, too.

     8   I'm not certain that the match starts at seven tomorrow, but I think *so / it*.

2   **Work in pairs. What does the correct word in each of 1–8 above refer back to?**

FOCUS: USING REFERENCE WORDS AS CLUES

3   **Match sentences 1–3 with sentences a–c to form a complete paragraph. Use reference words to help you.**

     1   If you've got a creative mind, why not invent something new?

     2   It's best to choose from subjects you already know quite a lot about.

     3   It's not enough just to have a brilliant idea.

     a   You also need to know how to make it work in practice.

     b   To do so, begin by deciding what you want to create.

     c   These could be things you've enjoyed studying at school or college.

4   **In pairs, underline the words and phrases that link the sentences in Exercise 3.**

Questions 16–20

Five sentences have been removed from the text below. For each question, choose the correct answer.
There are three extra sentences which you do not need to use.

Digging into the past

Last year, Kate Marshall was given a very exciting opportunity – to help her father, who's a history lecturer, at a historical site! He was leading a team to dig up and explore the area.

When they arrived, though, the site wasn't quite what Kate had expected.

16 [____] So the first job was to remove it all and prepare the land for digging. Says Kate, 'Dad hadn't warned me I'd have to work so hard as soon as we got there!'

But when the site was completely cleared, the team found pieces of ancient pots on the ground. However, those weren't as exciting as everyone had thought. Kate's dad told them that the important pots were still under the ground. And because no-one had touched them for centuries, the team would learn far more about their history – but first they would have to dig deeper. Says Kate, **17** [____] But we all knew Dad was right!'

The site was divided into small squares, with a leader for each square, who told everyone how to dig. 'That wasn't as easy as it sounded, either,' Kate reports. 'Instead of just digging great big holes, we all had to dig really carefully, and remove small amounts of soil each time. **18** [____] So it made sense.'

'My friends at home were really interested in what I was doing,' Kate explains. 'They kept texting me to ask what I'd found. **19** [____] But actually, we were looking for ordinary, everyday objects that could tell us about the people who'd lived in the area centuries ago.'

In the end, though, Kate wasn't disappointed by what she found. 'One day, when I was digging away, I found a stone with a strange shape. **20** [____] Someone had obviously made it hundreds of years ago, which meant it was really important. So Dad cleaned it up, and said it would go to the nearby museum. So I was pleased that at last, I'd found something interesting!'

A It turned out to be a small figure of a horse.

B No-one made that mistake, luckily.

C That way, everyone made sure they didn't miss anything.

D In fact, the whole area was actually still covered in grass.

E It was a bit sad to see it disappear.

F Some people were a bit disappointed by that news.

G They probably imagined it was things like gold jewellery.

H It was a new experience for me, too.

TIP Quickly read the main text and decide what each paragraph is about.

TIP Look for words in the main text and A–H that often link ideas, e.g. *this*, *too*.

In this part you:

- **read** a text with six gaps in it
- **choose** the correct word from four options for each gap

GRAMMAR: ADJECTIVES AND DEPENDENT PREPOSITIONS

1 Complete the table with the prepositions *of*, *about* and *with*.

Adjectives	Preposition
nervous, sad, worried, excited, crazy, sure	1 ....
frightened, fond, proud, jealous, ashamed	2 ....
disappointed, satisfied, fed up, impatient, bored	3 ....

FOCUS: USING PREPOSITIONS AND ADVERBS AS CLUES

👁 *B1 Preliminary* candidates often make mistakes with dependent prepositions and phrasal verbs.

2 **Find and correct the mistakes in these sentences.**

1 I've always been interested on science and I want to study biology at university.

2 As soon as the sun went out, the moon became very bright.

3 My brother isn't very keen of doing sport, but he loves watching it!

4 My mum was born in a small town, but she grew in London.

5 Some people are really afraid to snakes.

6 I don't know if I'll go swimming. It depends of what my friends want to do.

3 **Choose the best word (a, b, c or d) for each gap.**

1 In my school exam, I couldn't finish both essays because I .... out of time.

   a left   **b** ran   **c** got   **d** fell

2 Evie was .... with watching TV, so she started reading a book instead.

   a tired   **b** depressed   **c** bored   **d** stressed

3 We'll have to .... with that problem later. I don't have time right now.

   a look   **b** solve   **c** fix   **d** deal

4 I've always been really .... of small animals like rabbits.

   a keen   **b** friendly   **c** fond   **d** happy

5 I realised I couldn't .... off telling my parents the bad news any longer.

   a put   **b** wait   **c** delay   **d** leave

6 I was .... with my exam results. They were much better than I'd expected.

   a proud   **b** excited   **c** amazed   **d** delighted

> **Remember**
>
> A phrasal verb has two or more parts. The meaning of the phrasal verb is different from the meaning of the separate parts. (Example: *get on with someone* means *have a friendly relationship with someone*).

Questions 21–26

For each question, choose the correct answer.

 TIP Look at the words just before and just after each gap.

 TIP Try each of the 4 words in each gap. Which has the right meaning and also fits the grammar of the sentence?

Many cities have parks for people to enjoy. And it's very **(21)** .... to find wonderful sculptures in them. However, some sculptures found in Fairbanks, Alaska, aren't quite the same as in other cities. When the temperature **(22)** .... at the end of winter, they all disappear – because they're made of ice!

Fairbanks has been the home of the World Ice Art Championships for over 20 years, and artists from many different countries come to create spectacular ice sculptures. The ice is brought from a lake **(23)** .... near the sculpture park. It's said to be so clear that visitors can read a newspaper through it – even though the individual pieces are over one metre **(24)** .... !

Visitors also have the **(25)** .... to make their own ice sculptures if they wish, at special classes. There's a children's play park, too, where **(26)** .... everything is made of ice, including sculptures of favourite animals. It's a great place to visit!

21	A usual	B general	C common	D familiar
22	A develops	B rises	C grows	D builds
23	A located	B arranged	C contained	D attached
24	A heavy	B large	C strong	D thick
25	A occasion	B benefit	C opportunity	D ability
26	A totally	B absolutely	C completely	D fully

In this part you:

- **read** a text which has six gaps in it
- **write** one word to fill in each gap

FOCUS: READING FOR GIST

1 **Without trying to fill in any gaps, read the text below and answer these questions.**

What text type is it?

a a news report

b an article

c an advertisement

What is the writer's purpose?

a to encourage young people to study abroad

b to recommend a particular country

c to warn of the dangers of travelling

What is it about?

a the best way to travel

b the customs of other countries

c teenagers studying abroad

2 **In pairs, fill in gaps 1–4 using one word for each.**

For many young people, spending time as an exchange student abroad can be the **(1)** .... exciting experience of their lives. In **(2)** .... to being lots of fun, it helps teenagers learn about a different way of life as they get used **(3)** .... the customs in another country. They also become more confident when they realise that they can handle most problems on **(4)** .... own.

VOCABULARY: LINKING EXPRESSIONS

3 **Choose the correct linking words.**

1 Thomas went to bed very early *as / so* he was feeling sleepy.

2 OK, I'll lend you some money as *long / far* as you can pay me back.

3 There was nothing in the room *except / apart* from a table and chairs.

4 You'd better give me your number in *fact / case* I need to call you.

5 Turn off the tap when you brush your teeth in *future / order* to save water.

6 Let's go now *instead / in front* of waiting here all afternoon.

◉ *B1 Preliminary* candidates often make mistakes with linking words.

4 **Find and correct the mistakes in these sentences.**

1 Sienna's bike is much newer and better that mine.

2 We'll go for a picnic unless it doesn't rain.

3 I know I can always talk to my friend Lucy wherever I've got a problem.

4 Alfie bought some bread and too some apples.

5 I was late for school because the traffic.

6 Despite the train was full, I managed to find a seat.

Questions 27–32

For each question, write the correct word. Write **one** word for each gap.

 Begin Part 6 by quickly reading the whole text to find out what it's about.

 In some cases more than one word is possible for a gap, but you must only write one.

Hi Anna,

I've just been to the museum in our city. That was my first visit, believe it or **(27)** .... ! I wanted to collect some information for our class history project. We have to hand it **(28)** .... soon, don't we?

I went to the Ancient History section, **(29)** .... the museum keeps all its ancient Egyptian stuff. It was really interesting! There were some amazing statues of various animals, so I drew some pictures of them and then **(30)** .... some research about them online when I got home.

I've still got some work to do on my project, so I'll need to go back to the museum again some time soon. In fact, **(31)** .... don't we go together? I don't think you've been there before, **(32)** .... you? I'm sure you'll find something that you could use for your project.

See you soon!

Sally

In this part you:

- **read** an email with four notes attached
- **write** an answer to the email, using all the notes

FOCUS: UNDERSTANDING THE TASK

1 **In pairs, look at the Part 1 exam task on page 30 and answer the questions.**

   1 Who has written to you? *Jude, your English-speaking friend.*

   2 What is the email about?

   3 Find the four notes. What do they say?

   4 What kind of text are you going to write?

   5 How many words must you write?

2 **Match 1–7 in Jude's email with purposes a–g.**

   1 Do you like …

   2 See you soon, Jude

   3 Can your parents …

   4 What activities …

   5 Hi

   6 We want to set off …

   7 … coming to the beach with me …

   a finishing email and signing name

   b asking for information

   c starting an email

   d saying what the email is about

   e asking for suggestions

   f asking if something is possible

   g giving information

3 **Look at the notes in the email. In pairs, talk about the language you could use.**

   1 Me too!

   2 No, because …

   3 Explain which is better

   4 Suggest …

 TIP The notes pointing to parts of the email tell you what you must write about.

Remember

Always put the beginning, e.g. *Hi Jude*, the ending, e.g. *See you soon*, and your own name on separate lines.

 TIP You must include all the notes in your answer.

GRAMMAR: PREPOSITIONS OF TIME

4 **Circle the correct preposition in each sentence.**

1 We arrived *at / on* midday last Friday.

2 My sister often goes out *in / at* the evening.

3 Our school year finishes *on / in* June.

4 My grandparents are coming *on / in* Thursday.

5 The last bus is *on / at* 4.30.

6 *At / In* winter it gets very cold here.

7 My birthday is *in / on* 29th May.

8 My dad usually plays football *at / in* the weekend.

TIP
In Part 1, you may need to write times, days or dates. If so, use the right prepositions!

Remember

in January, *in* summer, *in* the morning, *in* the afternoon, *in* the evening, *at* the weekend, *at* night, *at* 5 p.m. *on* Monday, *on* 22nd May

VOCABULARY: MAKING SUGGESTIONS

5 **Complete the suggestions with words from the box.**

How about   Let's   Why don't we

1 .... go to the zoo on Saturday?

2 .... taking Sam to the beach for her birthday?

3 .... go to the cinema this evening.

4 .... take the train. It's quicker than the bus.

6 **Write a suggestion for each statement. The pictures will help you.**

1 I'm so hungry!
How about getting some food?

2 I'm so hot!

3 We're bored!

4 It's raining!

5 I don't know which bus to take!

You **must** answer this question.
Write your answer in about **100 words** on the answer sheet.

Question 1

Read this email from your English-speaking friend Jude and the notes you have made.

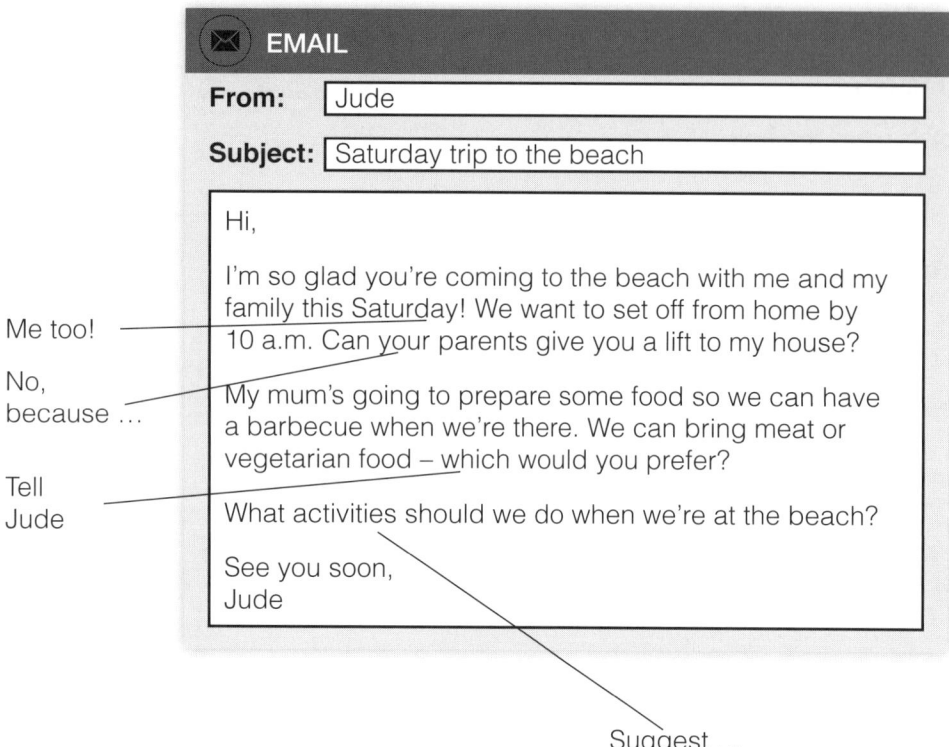

EMAIL

From: Jude

Subject: Saturday trip to the beach

Hi,

I'm so glad you're coming to the beach with me and my family this Saturday! We want to set off from home by 10 a.m. Can your parents give you a lift to my house?

My mum's going to prepare some food so we can have a barbecue when we're there. We can bring meat or vegetarian food – which would you prefer?

What activities should we do when we're at the beach?

See you soon,
Jude

Me too!

No, because …

Tell Jude

Suggest …

Advice

This task is always in an email format so you must start the email with an appropriate greeting, e.g. Dear (name), Hi (name), and an appropriate ending, e.g. Bye, See you soon, Best wishes, All the best,.

TIP As you will notice in this example writing task, there are lines that go to certain parts of the text. Pay special attention to where the lines are pointing and the notes at the other end of the lines (*Me too! / No, because … / Explain which is better / Suggest …*). The notes are telling you what you need to write about.

Write your **email** to Jude using **all the notes**.

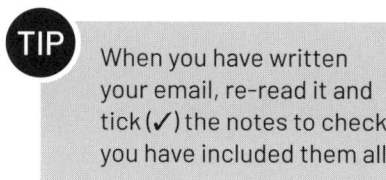

TIP When you have written your email, re-read it and tick (✓) the notes to check you have included them all.

In this part you:

- **choose** to write either an article or a story
- **write** a text of about 100 words

FOCUS: UNDERSTANDING THE TASK

1 In pairs, look at this exam task and answer questions **1–4**. You don't need to write the article.

> Write your answer in about **100 words** on the answer sheet.
> You see this notice on an English-language website for young people.
>
> **LEARNING** and the internet
>
> Write an article telling us whether the internet is the best place to look for information. Do you think only young people use the internet? What other ways are there to research new things?
>
> The best article will be published on our website.
>
> Write your **article.**

1 What do you have to write?

2 Who is asking you to write?

3 What is the topic?

4 How many words must you write?

FOCUS: STUDYING AN EXAMPLE ANSWER

2 In pairs, read Paulo's answer and answer questions **1–4**. (The numbers refer to Exercise 3.)

1 Has he answered all parts of the question correctly?

2 How does he give examples?

3 How does he give his opinions?

4 How could he improve his answer?

> In my opinion, the internet is probably the best place to [1] <u>look for</u> information, but I don't believe only [2] <u>young people</u> use it. For instance, my dad loves cooking and he's always [3] <u>looking for</u> new recipes so he can [4] <u>cook</u> different things, such as Indian meals. Also, my mum is keen on gardening and she [5] <u>uses the internet</u> all the time to get [6] <u>information</u> on topics like new plants.
>
> Although the internet is very useful, we can also [7] <u>research</u> new things in a library or ask at school. In my experience, teachers are always [8] <u>happy</u> to help their students learn more.

VOCABULARY: USING DIFFERENT WORDS

3 Replace the underlined words in Paulo's answer with words with similar meanings from the box.

TIP When you write your article try to use your own words, don't just repeat the words in the question.

teenagers	make	find out about	willing
goes online	try to find	details	searching for

FOCUS: GIVING EXAMPLES

4 Complete the sentences with words from the box.

> like   as   instance   for

1 Technology has changed the world in many different ways. Washing machines and dishwashers, ... example, make our lives easier.

2 Spanish is spoken in many countries, such .... Argentina, Colombia and Mexico.

3 There are many ways to save money, ... buying second-hand clothes and eating out less.

4 Climate change is affecting the world's weather; nowadays there are more storms, for ....

FOCUS: GIVING OPINIONS

5 Listen to Ben and Katy. They are talking about watching TV. Match the person with their opinions. Label the statements (a–f) with B (Ben) or K (Katy).

a thinks most programmes are OK

b would rather watch films on a computer

c believes there are lots of good films on TV

d doesn't like watching sports on TV

e agrees there are some funny programmes

f enjoyed watching a documentary

Ben   Katy

6 Complete the dialogue from Exercise 5 with words from the box. Then listen and check.

> Personally, I think   hate   In my opinion   To be honest
> suppose   love   interested in   That's true

Katy: Hi Ben. Did you see the documentary last night about the Olympic Games? It was brilliant. I learned so much.

Ben: Did you? I thought it was quite boring, but I'm not really **(1)** .... sports programmes.

Katy: But you **(2)** .... sports. You play football and tennis and basketball and …

Ben: Yes, I enjoy playing sports, but I **(3)** .... watching them on TV.

Katy: Oh, so what kind of TV programmes do you like?

Ben: **(4)** ...., I don't watch much TV. I prefer watching films on my laptop. **(5)** ...., TV isn't very good.

Katy: I don't agree. **(6)** .... you can see plenty of good films and some really funny shows, too.

Ben: **(7)** .... I did see a good comedy on Friday night, but most programmes are rubbish!

Katy: I **(8)** .... there are some bad programmes, but only a few.

Choose **one** of these questions.
Write your answer in about **100 words** on the answer sheet.

....

Question 2

You see this notice in your school English-language magazine.

Articles wanted!
FRIENDSHIP
Write an article telling us how important it is for friends to have similar characters.
Do you think it's better to have lots of friends or just one best friend? Why?
The best articles answering these questions will be published next month.

Write your **article**.

 TIP For each point you make in your article, try to give an example or two.

 TIP Check your completed article includes all the points in the question.

 TIP Make sure you answer the Writing questions in about 100 words about the topic.

TIP You should talk about your personal experience when writing the article. If you think about your own personal experiences related to the topic, this may help you when you are planning what to write.

Question 3

Your English teacher has asked you to write a story. Your story must begin with this sentence:

Morgan couldn't wait any longer to see what was inside the ancient box.

Write your **story**.

In this part you:

- **listen** to one or two people talking about seven short situations
- **match** what they say with a picture

TIP In Part 1, you will hear recordings on familiar topics such as free time, school, travel and animals. It is a good idea to learn words related to these topics.

VOCABULARY: TOPICS

1 Circle the word which is different in each group. There may be more than one possible answer.

1 ferry	helicopter	spaceship	aeroplane
2 lion	giraffe	elephant	sheep
3 windsurfing	football	rugby	hockey
4 chemistry	biology	history	physics
5 swimming	skiing	knitting	dancing
6 stadium	gym	factory	athletics track
7 French	Spain	German	Italian
8 racket	coach	bat	surfboard

2 Explain why the words you chose are different. The words in the box may be helpful.

country	work	team	water
science	active	wild	equipment

3 Choose the best word from Exercise 1 for each gap.

1 I go .... in the mountains every winter. I wear a helmet and thick clothes.

2 One of my favourite team sports at the Winter Olympics is ice-............................ .

3 My grandmother loves .... She made this pair of gloves for me.

4 The .... is a meat-eating animal which can be dangerous to humans.

5 You can catch a .... across to the island every hour.

6 I need a new tennis .... Mine is broken.

7 I'm really bad at .... I can never remember important dates!

FOCUS: SUGGESTIONS AND RESPONSES

4 In Part 1, speakers sometimes suggest things to do, buy or eat. Match the suggestions to the responses.

1	Let's play football.	a	We had that yesterday.
2	Why don't we take a picnic?	b	That's far too early!
3	I suggest we get him a book.	c	Car might be quicker.
4	We should meet at 4.	d	I can't. I've hurt my ankle.
5	Why not go by train?	e	Yes, good idea. He loves reading.
6	How about getting pizza?	f	Ooh, I love eating outside!

 TIP If you hear a suggestion, listen for the response. Does the other speaker accept or reject the suggestion?

5 Listen to the dialogue. Which subject do they decide to study first?

A

B

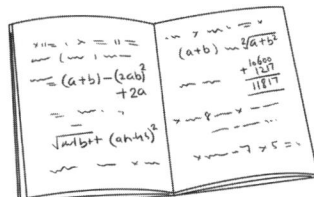

C

6 Listen again and choose the correct response.

1 Why don't they start with maths?
   a They might need help with it.
   b It's not due in tomorrow.

2 Why don't they start with geography?
   a They have more time.
   b They don't have to write much.

3 Why do they decide to start with science?
   a They understand it well.
   b It's more urgent.

7 Use the pictures to make suggestions and respond to your partner's suggestions.

Example

How about watching a film tonight at my house?
That's a nice idea, but I've got football training. / Great idea – what film do you fancy?

A

B

C

TIP Read the questions and look at all of the pictures carefully before you listen.

Questions 1–7

03 For each question, choose the correct answer.

1 What is the girl going to bring for the picnic?

A

B

C

2 Which activity did the boy enjoy most during his holiday?

A

B

C

3 What homework does the girl have to do tonight?

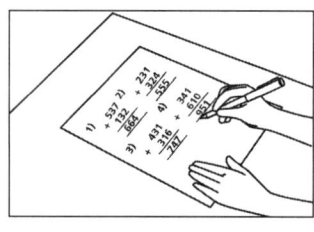

A

B

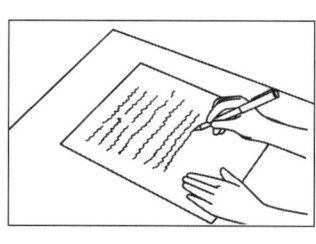

C

4   Where did the students go on their school trip?

A

B

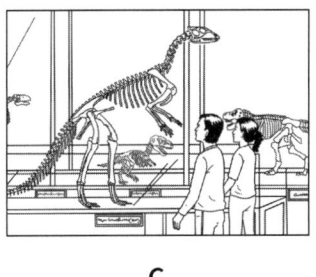

C

5   Which present has the boy already bought?

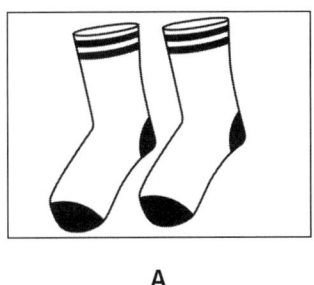

A

B

C

6   Where did the boy go with his family at the weekend?

A

B

C

7   How will the girl get to her friend's house?

A

B

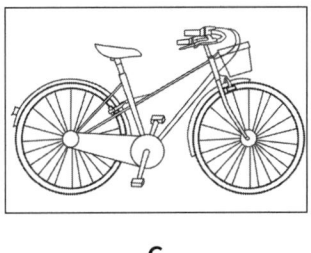

C

In this part you:

- **listen** to two speakers talking about a topic
- **answer** six multiple-choice questions

VOCABULARY: ADJECTIVES

1 Match a word from column A with a word with a similar meaning from column B and a word with the opposite meaning from column C.

A	B	C
scary	lovely	narrow
wide	frightening	normal
dull	huge	calming
strange	complicated	tiny
enormous	boring	nasty
pleasant	odd	simple
hard	broad	exciting

2 Listen and decide which word from Exercise 1 has been replaced by a 'bleep'. There may be more than one possible answer.

1 .... 2 .... 3 .... 4 .... 5 ....

FOCUS: AGREEING AND DISAGREEING

3 Read the dialogues and write A (agree) or D (disagree).

1 Oh, look at that painting. It's so beautiful!
  But the colours are so dull!

2 The food on the plane was disgusting.
  I actually quite enjoyed it.

3 Frankie is such a talented singer.
  Absolutely!

4 The Star Wars films are absolutely brilliant!
  If you like that kind of thing …

5 Chemistry is the most difficult subject we have this year.
  I couldn't agree more.

6 Mobile phones should not be allowed in schools.
  Exactly!

4 Listen and choose the correct option.

You hear two friends talking about what cake to buy for their friend's birthday. Which cake do they decide to buy?

A chocolate

B strawberry

C plain

Questions 8–13

For each question, choose the correct answer.

8   You will hear two friends talking about a film they've just seen.
    Why didn't the boy enjoy the film?
    A   It was very frightening.
    B   It lasted too long.
    C   It had terrible acting.

9   You will hear two friends talking about some biology homework.
    The girl suggests that the boy should
    A   ask his teacher for help.
    B   get information from the internet.
    C   look in the biology textbook.

> **Advice**
>
> *9 What does the girl say about the internet? What does she suggest the boy does with the textbook? Does this advice match option C?*

10 You will hear two friends talking about an interview with a singer they've seen on TV.
    They agree that
    A   the singer's answers were interesting.
    B   the interviewer was quite rude.
    C   the questions were confusing.

11 You will hear a girl telling her friend about a diving trip.
    How did the girl feel about it?
    A   sure she will go again
    B   glad she went with a relative
    C   pleased with her diving skills

> **Advice**
>
> *11 Does the girl say she was good at diving when she tried it in the sea? What does she say about the relative she went with?*

12 You will hear a girl talking to a friend about basketball.
    The girl is trying to
    A   explain the rules of the game.
    B   describe a game she took part in.
    C   encourage the boy to start playing.

13 You will hear a boy talking about a trip to a city with his family.
    Why did the boy's family get lost?
    A   They couldn't understand their map.
    B   Someone gave them the wrong directions.
    C   The guidebook contained incorrect information.

In this part you:

- **listen**   to one person talking about a topic
- **complete** some notes about the topic

FOCUS: LINKING WORDS AND PHRASES AND ADVERBIALS

1   **Link the two parts of the sentences. Use the words and phrases in bold to help you.**

1	**Unfortunately,**	a	Pierre has a part-time job.
2	India is **second only to**	b	the bus stop's just outside my house.
3	**Instead of** ordering the soup,	c	**However,** I don't speak much French.
4	I grew up in France.	d	it's going to rain tomorrow.
5	I ski every winter	e	China as a producer of tea.
6	**Luckily,**	f	shall we have salad?
7	**As well as** studying,	g	**although** I'm not very good.

> **TIP** In the Listening test, pay attention to linking words and expressions as they can affect the meaning.

2   **Choose the best linking words or phrases or adverbs in bold from Exercise 1 to go in each gap.**

1   Germany was .... Norway in the medals table.

2   Rashmin usually wears smart clothes. ...., today he's dressed casually.

3   We're going camping tomorrow. ...., the weather is improving.

4   .... I don't usually like action films, I quite enjoyed that one.

5   .... playing tennis for her club, Gemma is an excellent swimmer.

6   You should go for a walk .... watching TV every evening.

FOCUS: PREDICTING ANSWERS

3   **You are going to hear a teacher talking to some students about a school trip to an aquarium. In each gap, write one or two words or a number or a date or a time.**

07   **Before listening, decide what kind of information you need to listen for.**

> **TIP** Read the instructions carefully and think about the type of information needed in a gap before you listen.

1   Cost of entry to the aquarium: £...................................

2   Students need to bring: ....

3   Sharks feeding time: .... p.m.

4   11 a.m. talk about: ....

Now listen and complete the gaps.

4   **The teacher now gives some more information about the aquarium. Listen for the spellings and write down the information.**

08   **Name of aquarium:** Aquarina

1   **Address:** .... Road

2   **Name of guide:** Sarah ....

Questions 14–19

09 For each question, write the correct answer in the gap.
Write **one** or **two words** or a **number** or a **date** or a **time**.

TIP Read each piece of information in the box below and try and guess possible answers for each gap.

You will hear a student giving a review of a new video game to his class.

Video game review

Action takes place in:	a **(14)** ....
Players answer questions about:	**(15)** ....
Name of most difficult level of game:	the **(16)** ....
Best thing about the game:	the **(17)** ....
Maximum number of players:	**(18)** ....
Website for more details:	www.**(19)** .... .com

Advice

(14) Where does the action take place in video games you know? Can you imagine any other places?

In this part you:

- **listen**   to an interview
- **choose**   the correct answer (A, B or C) from six multiple-choice questions

GRAMMAR: TIME PHRASES

1   **Put one word in each gap.**

> for   since   ago

1   I went on holiday to Japan three years ....
2   Jenna has been in the photography club .... 2015.
3   I've been playing for the school team .... six months.

Make some sentences about yourself using *for*, *since* and *ago*.

2   **Listen to a girl called Silvia talking about her life and answer the questions.**

1   Where does Silvia live now?
- **a**   China
- **b**   London
- **c**   Rome

2   Silvia's Mum became interested in learning Chinese
- **a**   before she went to China.
- **b**   while she lived in China.
- **c**   after she left China.

3   Silvia's brother is now in
- **a**   Rome.
- **b**   London.
- **c**   China.

3   **Anita is a 16-year-old girl who helps out at a home for stray cats. Listen and put the events in the correct order.**

- **a**   Anita cleaned the cats' cages.
- **b**   Anita started helping the vet.
- **c**   Anita started visiting Cat Rescue.
- **d**   Anita's mum started volunteering at Cat Rescue.
- **e**   Anita started helping at Cat Rescue.

TIP   Listen for time phrases as they can help you understand the order of events.

TIP   Understanding time phrases and tenses can help while you listen and when answering the exam questions.

Remember

She has (She's) worked there for 2 years = she works there now.
She worked there for 2 years = this happened in the past – she doesn't work there now.

Questions 20–25

For each question, choose the correct answer.

You will hear an interview with a 15-year-old girl called Andrea, who plays ice hockey for her National Under-16s Team.

20 Which sport does Andrea say she started playing first?

A   football

B   ice hockey

C   basketball

21 Andrea says that she first started playing ice hockey after

A   watching a family member play.

B   seeing a game on television.

C   talking about it with her friends.

> **Advice**
>
> 21 Did Andrea like ice hockey after seeing her brother play? What does she say about her friends? Does this match with option C?

22 Why does Andrea think that playing against boys is important?

A   It improves her own playing skills.

B   It proves there are many girls playing the sport.

C   It increases respect for female players.

23 How did Andrea feel when she was chosen for the national under-16s team?

A   surprised to be asked

B   sorry to leave her club

C   confident in her abilities

> **Advice**
>
> 23 What does Andrea say about her abilities? What does she say about being chosen for the team? Was she surprised?

24 Andrea's favourite games are those which are

A   easy to win.

B   shown on TV.

C   exciting to watch.

25 Andrea says that people who want to start playing ice hockey should

A   find a club.

B   buy good equipment.

C   learn the rules.

Training Test 1 | Speaking Part 1

In this part of the test you will:

- **talk**   to an interlocutor for 2–3 minutes
- **answer**   some general questions about you and your family

FOCUS: PERSONAL QUESTIONS

1 Answer these questions about yourself.

1 What's your name? ....
2 How old are you? ....
3 Where do you live? ....
4 Who do you live with? ....

> **TIP**
> In Phase 2 of this part of the Speaking test, be ready to talk about your past experiences and future plans, as well as about the present.

2 Match these Phase 2 questions and answers.

1 When do you practise speaking English?

2 How long have you studied English for?

3 Which other languages would you like to learn?

4 What do you usually do when you're with your friends?

5 How did you meet your best friend?

6 What plans do you have for your next school holiday?

7 What did you do last night?

a I think it would be really useful to learn Chinese, but I think it would be very difficult.

b We were in the same class when we started secondary school. We were 11 years old.

c For about five years now.

d I did some homework, had dinner then watched TV with my family.

e In my English classes and also sometimes with my friends after class.

f I am going to visit my grandparents, who live in Madrid.

g We play video games together or sometimes go out to the cinema or park.

3 Now ask and answer the questions in Exercise 2 with a partner.

FOCUS: LISTENING

4 Listen and complete the interlocutor's questions.

13

1 .... kinds of TV programmes do you enjoy ....?
2 .... us about the area .... you live.
3 What do you .... do after ....?
4 Where .... you go last ....?
5 What are you .... to do ....?

(2–3 minutes)

Phase 1
Interlocutor

To A/B Good morning / afternoon / evening.
Can I have your mark sheets, please?
Hand over the mark sheets to the assessor.

To A/B I'm .... and this is ....

To A What's your name? How old are you?
Thank you.

To B And what's your name? How old are you?
Thank you.

To B **B**, where do you live?
Who do you live with?
Thank you.

To A And **A**, where do you live?
Who do you live with?
Thank you.

TIP Listen carefully to the interlocutor's questions, and ask if there's something you don't understand.

TIP There will be two examiners in the room. The person who asks you questions is the interlocutor. The other person is the assessor, who sits further away and makes notes, and doesn't speak. If there's anything you don't understand, ask the interlocutor, who will be happy to explain.

Phase 2
Interlocutor

The interlocutor may ask you one or more of the following questions.

Tell us about your best friend.

How often do you use the internet?

What do you usually do in the evening?

What is your favourite school subject? (Why?)

Which TV programmes do you enjoy watching? (Why?)

Do you like playing or watching any sports? (Why? / Why not?)

What's your favourite kind of music? (Why?)

Tell us about your bedroom.

Advice

Practise asking and answering these questions with a friend. This will help you feel confident right from the beginning of the test.

 Listen to two students answering some of the questions above.
14

In this part of the test you will:

- **talk** to the interlocutor about a colour photograph
- **describe** what you can see in the photograph

VOCABULARY: DESCRIBING PEOPLE, THINGS AND PLACES

1   Where are you now? What can you see? Who can you see? What are they doing? Try to describe the room you are in, what you can see there and the people around you in as much detail as you can.

2   Look at the photograph below. What can you see? Who are the people? Where are they? What are they doing? Describe what you can see in as much detail as you can.

3   Listen to a student describing this photograph. Does she say the same things you said about the people? What does she say about the place?

15

> ### Remember
>
> Use the present simple, especially *there is* and *there are* to describe the photograph in general and the things you can see, e.g. *The photo shows a school library. There are lots of shelves.* Use the present continuous to describe what the people are doing and wearing, e.g. *The students are all wearing school uniforms. They are sitting at a table.*

> ### Remember
>
> Use phrases like these to say where things are.
> - *In the middle of the photograph, there is...*
> - *On the back of the chair, there is...*
> - *Behind the students, there are...*
> - *On the shelves, there are....*
> Can you think of any more phrases?

(3–5 minutes)

Interlocutor

> Now I'd like each of you to talk on your own about something. I'm going to give each of you a photograph and I'd like you to talk about it.
>
> **A**, here is your photograph. It shows someone **doing her homework.**

The interlocutor will place Exam Practice Test 1 Speaking Part 2 picture (see page C1), in front of Candidate A.

> **B**, you just listen. **A**, please tell us what you can see in the photograph.

Candidate A

(Approximately 1 minute)

Interlocutor

> Thank you.

Back-up prompts (for **A** and **B**)
- Talk about the person/people.
- Talk about the place.
- Talk about other things in the photograph.

Interlocutor

> **B**, here is your photograph. It shows some people **getting their lunch.**

The interlocutor will place Exam Practice Test 1 Speaking Part 2 picture (see page C2), in front of Candidate B.

Interlocutor

> **A**, you just listen. **B**, please tell us what you can see in the photograph.

Candidate B

(Approximately 1 minute)

Interlocutor

> Thank you.

   Listen to a student talking about Photos A, B and C. (See pages C1, C2 and C7.)

16 17 18

In this part of the test you will:

- **look at** information the interlocutor gives you
- **discuss** your views and opinions with your partner

FOCUS: MAKING SUGGESTIONS, AGREEING AND DISAGREEING

1 A school wants to have a cookery competition for students and needs to choose a suitable prize for the winner. Look at the four possible prizes and listen to Gina and Harry talking about them. Which prize does Gina think is best? Why? Does Harry agree with Gina? Why not? Which prize do they agree on in the end?

> **Remember**
>
> There are lots of phrases you can use for making suggestions: *Why don't they ...? How about ...? I think the school should ...*
> *I think the X would be the best prize because ...*

2 Read Gina and Harry's conversation, then listen again and complete the text with words from the recording.

H: So which prize do you think they should give, Gina?

G: Hmm ... I think the chef's hat **(1)** .... Only cooks and chefs wear hats like that. It's so unusual, and I'd love to have something like that.

H: I **(2)** .... that. The person who wins will definitely be a teenager and probably just enjoys cooking as a hobby. They're not a professional chef, so I don't think it will be very useful. **(3)** .... the cake? Everyone likes cake.

G: I don't! And it's not a very healthy prize either! **(4)** .... they give the pans then? **(5)** .... about that?

H: I think their parents have probably got lots of pans already.

G: **(6)** .... right, but they might not have any up-to-date cookery books, and they're a great way of learning how to cook better, too.

H: **(7)** ....! Yes, they're definitely the best prize.

3 Which prize do you think would be best for the winner of a school cookery competition? Discuss this with your partner.

> **TIP**
>
> Choose the pictures that you think will be easiest to talk about and discuss those ones first.

4 A boy wants to buy a present for his older sister who has just got her driving licence. Discuss these ideas for a present in pairs.

 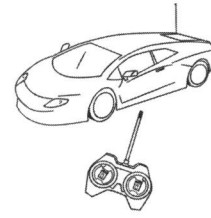  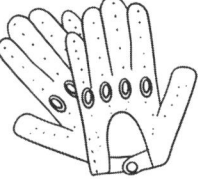

Exam Practice Test 1 — Speaking Part 3

(4–5 minutes)

Advice

What can you do on a laptop on a long journey? Do you like reading? How long do you usually read for? Do you think playing games is fun? Can you spend a few hours listening to music?

Interlocutor

Now, in this part of the test you're going to talk about something together for about two minutes. I'm going to describe a situation to you.

The interlocutor will place Exam Practice Test 1 Speaking Part 2 set of pictures (see page C11), in front of both candidates.

Interlocutor

A girl is going on a long bus journey with her family to visit some relatives. She can take one thing with her on the bus for entertainment during the journey.

Here are some things she could take with her.

Talk together about the different things she could take with her, and say which would be best.

All right? Now talk together.

(Approximately 2–3 minutes)

Interlocutor

Thank you.

Listen to two students doing the task above.

20

In this part of the test you will:

- **answer** questions on a similar topic to Part 3
- **give** your views and opinions to your partner and the interlocutor

FOCUS: GIVING YOUR OPINION

1 Listen to Theo and Lidia giving their opinions about the foods they like. Complete the text with words from the recording.

Theo

The food I really like is pizza. I think it's really **(1)** .... whatever you put on top of it and I like lots of **(2)** .... of pizza. I think **(3)** ...., though, is chicken and pineapple. I know it sounds a bit strange, but it tastes **(4)** ....! It's because the pineapple is sweet and the chicken and cheese isn't, so they go really well together. **(5)** .... you, Lidia? What food **(6)** .... like?

Lidia

I like pizza **(7)** ...., but the food I like most is ice cream **(8)** .... I can buy it in so many nice flavours and I **(9)** .... all of them. I **(10)** .... chocolate and vanilla rather than strawberry or other fruit flavours, **(11)** .... I'm very happy to eat them all! I think that learning how to make ice cream **(12)** .... really interesting. Do you like making pizzas, Theo?

2 Now listen to the second part of Theo and Lidia's conversation about healthy and unhealthy foods. Complete the phrases for agreeing and disagreeing.

Theo: I think fast food is really bad for you.

Lidia: **(1)**................... Most fast food restaurants and takeaways sell salads and things like that. **(2)**................... that a lot of the things we think about when we mention fast food, like burgers and chips, aren't good for you, but other things aren't so bad.

Theo: **(3)**................... I think that even if you have a burger every now and then, it's not going to do you any harm. It's when you eat them every day it becomes a problem.

Lidia: **(4)**................... Some scientists think that things like chocolate are good for you, too.

Theo: **(5)**................... only if you eat a very small amount each day.

TIP Look at your partner when you're talking to them. This helps to give both of you confidence.

Remember

It's really important to respond to what your partner or the interlocutor says, to keep the conversation moving forward. You can use words and phrases like *That's sounds amazing/great/wonderful/lovely/awful/terrible!... That's right ... Do you? ... Really?*

Remember

There are lots of phrases you can use for agreeing and disagreeing
- agreeing: *That's a good idea! ... I agree ... I think so too ... Me too! ... I guess so ... Exactly! That's true!*
- disagreeing: *I'm not sure that ... I don't think ... I don't agree ... I'm not so sure ... Yes, but ... No, but ...*

3 Take turns to read out questions (**1–6**) below. Respond to what your partner says with one of the phrases in speech bubbles. Keep the conversation going by then asking another question on the topic.

> Me neither!   Are you? I'm not!   So do I!   Me too!   Really? That'd be great!   Don't you? I do!

1 I much prefer pasta to rice.
2 I think a holiday by the beach is the best kind of holiday.
3 I'd love to go to New York.
4 I don't really like comedy films. They never make me laugh.
5 I'm really frightened of travelling on aeroplanes.
6 I'd like to design my own jewellery.

Exam Practice Test 1   Speaking Part 4

(3–4 minutes)

Interlocutor
(to both candidates)

- Have you ever been on a really long journey? (Where did you go?)
- Which do you prefer, travelling by car or travelling by bus? (Why?)
- Have you ever been on an aeroplane? (Did you enjoy it?)
- Do you like travelling by train? (Why? / Why not?)
- Is it important for people to think about the environment when they choose how to travel? (Why? / Why not?)

Thank you. That is the end of the test.

Listen to two students doing the task above.

23

Advice

Which do you prefer, travelling by car or travelling by bus? Think about:
- *how comfortable each type of transport is.*
- *how fast each type of transport is.*
- *how convenient each type of transport is.*
- *how expensive each type of transport is.*

- How many texts do you have to read in Part 1?
- What do you have to decide when you look at A, B and C?

FOCUS: WORDS WITH SIMILAR MEANING

1   Match expressions 1–5 with the expressions a–e that have similar meanings.

1   Photography is not permitted in the art gallery.
2   The swimming pool will no longer be open after 8 p.m.
3   The printer was bought recently and works perfectly.
4   If the side entrance is closed, please use the main entrance.
5   Discount for under-12s when accompanied by a parent.

a   It is changing its opening hours.
b   It's in good condition and is almost new.
c   Lower prices for some children if they are with their mother or father.
d   You must not use your camera here.
e   You may have to go in a different way.

FOCUS: TEXT TYPES, CONTEXT AND FUNCTION

2   Look at the six short texts. Match 1–6 with text types a–f and say where you might see them.

a   email   b   label   c   advertisement   d   note   e   notice   f   road sign

1
These doors must be kept open at all times.

2
Wash sweater by hand only, at low temperature.

3
New Message

Hi Molly
I hope you're coming to see us next month! You should book your train tickets quickly if you are.
Alice

4

No motor vehicles allowed in this part of the village

5
Mum,
I'm a little short of cash. Can you lend me a bit until the weekend? Back home soon.
Isabelle

6

LEARN TO COOK
for just **£20** a week!
First lesson free if you register by this Friday.

3   Match answers a–f with short texts 1–6 in Exercise 2.

a   You must not drive here.
b   You don't have to pay for your first class if you join before the weekend.
c   Do not put in washing machine or use hot water.
d   She ought to make travel arrangements soon if she's going to visit.
e   She hasn't got much money and wants to borrow some.
f   Do not close them for any reason.

GRAMMAR: IMPERATIVES AND 'NO + –ING' FORMS

4 Complete the orders with words from the box.

> standing   put on   stop   running
> use   camping

1 .... here when traffic lights are red.
2 No .... in the nature park.
3 .... this exit when film ends.
4 No .... near the driver or the doors.
5 No .... on the stairs.
6 .... your seatbelts for landing.

Remember

We give instructions or commands with imperative verbs: *Listen! Don't talk!*
We can also tell someone <u>not</u> to do something with *no + -ing*: *No parking on the grass.*

5 Where would you see orders 1–6 from Exercise 4? Match them with a–f below.

a in a cinema
b in the countryside
c on a plane
d in the street
e inside a school building
f on a bus

Remember

We can say *allow someone <u>to</u> do something* or *let someone do something* (without *to*).

6 In pairs, complete 1–6 using the correct form of suitable verbs.

1 .... right at the end of this road.

2 No ....
Dangerous rocks in water.

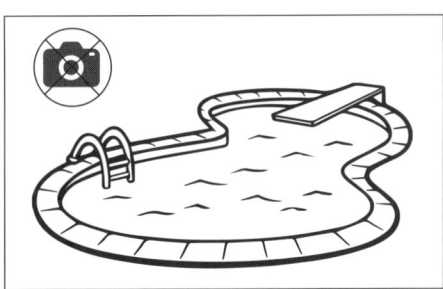

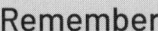

3 Please don't .... photos in the swimming pool area.

4 No .... in this park except at weekends.

5 .... passengers leave the train before you board.

6 No ....
in this area.

Questions 1–5

For each question, choose the correct answer.

1

HEAVY SNOW EXPECTED OVERNIGHT TRAIN AND BUS DELAYS POSSIBLE CHECK WEBSITES REGULARLY – SOME SCHOOLS AND OFFICES MAY BE CLOSED TOMORROW

A   The bad weather will make a lot of public transport late tomorrow.

B   Snow that is falling will cause a number of problems tomorrow.

C   Students should watch for announcements in case they are unable to attend classes tomorrow.

2

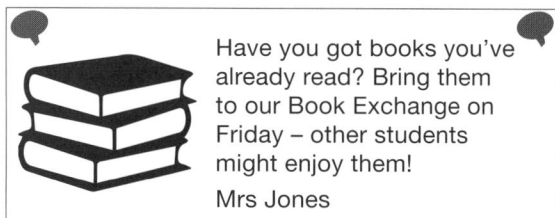

Have you got books you've already read? Bring them to our Book Exchange on Friday – other students might enjoy them!
Mrs Jones

What is Mrs Jones asking students to do?

A   share books they no longer want with their schoolmates

B   find out from other students which books they've enjoyed

C   bring in a good book to talk about on Friday

3

Billy,
Have you got Joanna's number? I'm supposed to meet her at the cinema in 10 minutes, but Dad's driving me into town and we're in a huge traffic jam! Thanks!
Sophie

A   Sophie wants Billy to contact Joanna and warn her about traffic problems in town.

B   Sophie needs to let Joanna know that she's probably going to be late.

C   Sophie's not sure when she's supposed to meet Joanna to see a film.

4

New Message

From: Coach

To: Rugby club

Just wanted to thank players in Saturday's match, and people who supported them. Remember, the other side were league winners, so all wasn't bad – but next time let's beat them!

What is the coach doing?

A congratulating the team on their most recent win

B letting the team's fans know the positive effect of their support

C encouraging the team to play even better in a future match

5

Café Menu

See below for our regular dishes – or for today's 'specials' go inside to see the board by the counter!

A We have more food available, apart from what's written on the menu.

B To decide what to eat, you must go and look at the board inside.

C Speak to someone at the counter when you want to order your food.

 TIP When you have chosen A, B or C, compare it with the text and check that it really says the same thing.

- How many descriptions of people do you have to read in Part 2?
- How many matching texts can you choose from?

FOCUS: IDENTIFYING KEY WORDS

1 Complete the text with words from the box.

| rather | stand | mind | fancy | prefer | fond | keen |

Sonia doesn't **(1)** .... going abroad because she isn't **(2)** .... on travelling long distances and she really can't **(3)** .... flying. She would **(4)** .... to have a holiday near her home and she'd **(5)** .... go camping than stay in a hotel. She's **(6)** .... of nature and really doesn't **(7)** .... if it rains a lot!

2 Work in pairs. Which of the words in Exercise 1 do we use for something we:

a like? **b** prefer? **c** dislike? **d** don't think is important?

👁 *B1 Preliminary* candidates often make mistakes with words that express likes and dislikes.

FOCUS: IDENTIFYING LIKES, DISLIKES AND PREFERENCES

3 Read this description of someone who wants to go to a sports centre. Underline the key expressions and the words that tell you what he likes and prefers.

Ethan wants to train every day and he doesn't mind paying a regular amount to stay fit. He fancies learning a new sport and prefers to make reservations by email.

FOCUS: MATCHING KEY WORDS WITH PARAPHRASES

4 Read these descriptions of three sports centres and decide which of A–C would be the most suitable for Ethan. Then say why that is the correct answer.

A Greenfields

We don't charge much: just a £3 entrance fee (free for students). In summer, relax in our outdoor pool or walk around our beautiful gardens. Open Tuesday to Friday, plus weekends. We care about the environment, so please don't bring your car.

B Topfitness

There's nowhere better to get really fit. Gym membership costs just £20 per month and our squash courts can be reserved online. Lessons are available for most activities. We open from 7 a.m. to 10 p.m. daily; hot and cold drinks are available.

C Eastpark

Eastpark has both outdoor and indoor pools, playing areas for football and rugby and a first-class gym. Facilities can be booked by phone only. For students, we offer reduced prices for membership. There are bus stops nearby and parking is free.

TIP Remember that for each of descriptions 6–10 only one of A–H is correct, so there are three texts you will not use.

Questions 6–10

For each question, choose the correct answer.

The people below all want to visit a studio where films are made.
On the next page there are descriptions of eight film studios that people can visit.
Decide which film studios would be the most suitable for the people below.

 6  Tom wants to look around the studio at his own speed, and visit the actual sets where films were made. His mum wants to see online what the studio is like before she buys tickets.

 7  Ingrid is interested in seeing costumes that famous actors have worn, and she'd also like to ride on a vehicle that originally appeared in a film. Ingrid's mum wants a souvenir to remember their trip.

 8  Roberto wants to visit a studio where famous films were made many years ago, and buy something that appeared in one of the films. His dad wants to book online before they go.

 9  Simone likes science fiction films, and prefers looking at digital displays about how special effects are achieved to reading information. Simone's dad wants to get a digital guide.

 10  Ben is interested in how scenes from famous cities are created in studios. He'd also like to visit film locations outside the studios, accompanied by a guide who can answer his questions.

Film studios

A   Grand Studios

These studios have been the home of special effects for years! There's plenty to look at and read, so allow lots of time for your visit. And our friendly guides around the studios are ready to help direct you to the most interesting sights. It's best to book online in advance.

B   Movieworld

You'll find the best movies ever here, set far into the future! Use the interactive videos on our computers, to see how actors are turned into on-screen monsters, using amazing make-up, costumes and filming techniques, and models of dinosaurs are created to look as though they're alive! There are video activities, and 'tours' of the studio to download.

C   Waverley Studios

These studios are huge, with plenty of space for displaying the scenery and stages where big stars acted in scenes from famous films. Check the website to see exactly what the studio offers inside. And because you're not shown around in groups, you can spend as much time there as you want!

D   Screen World

Many famous movies from the last century were made in these studios, and you can still see the costumes worn in them, and the original sets used in the films. There's a useful digital guide you can buy here, so you'll find your way through these studios really quickly!

E   WestWays

To visit this studio, get tickets in advance through the website, to avoid long queues – it's very popular with people who love top movies from the 40s, many of which were filmed here. The studio also has a great selection of items from various movies, now on sale as souvenirs!

F   FilmFun

Come and visit amazingly realistic sets, from the streets of New York to the historical sites of Rome – and walk around them! The tour also includes a bus ride to places in the surrounding area which have appeared in films, with a staff member to tell you whatever you'd like to know.

G   Star Studios

See a 360° online tour of these studios before you come – they're huge! And during your visit, ride through what look like London and Paris streets, on original buses used in old films, and even try on costumes from films made here. Digital displays will give you plenty of information!

H   FilmPark

FilmPark has an amazing collection of old cars once used in films – and they still work! So, have a trip in one and see the studios as you're driven around its huge city street scenes. There's also a collection of original clothes that stars were dressed in for their movies. Visitors get free photos of themselves as they leave.

- Is there a short text for each question, or one long text?
- How many options are there for each question?

VOCABULARY: ATTITUDE AND OPINION ADJECTIVES

1 **We often use these adjectives to describe attitude and opinion. Use one of them to say how each of the people in 1–8 feels.**

| ashamed | cheerful | confident | grateful | jealous | impressed | patient | upset |

1 Thanks very much for helping me. You're very kind.
2 I've been in a good mood all day!
3 I've studied really hard, so I'm sure I'll do well in tomorrow's test.
4 It was silly of me to do that. I'm very sorry.
5 I thought my team would win the cup, but they lost the final 5–0!
6 I can't believe that's the first time you skated! You did so well!
7 You can take as much time as you like. I'll wait here for you.
8 It's not fair: that boy's got a much newer phone than me!

GRAMMAR: –ED AND –ING ATTITUDE AND OPINION ADJECTIVES

2 **Choose the correct form of the adjectives.**

1 I was very *interesting / interested* in what that woman said about music.
2 That was probably the most *bored / boring* TV show I've ever seen.
3 I was *disappointed / disappointing* that my friends couldn't go to the fair with me.
4 The ending of that film was really *shocked / shocking*. It kept me awake last night!
5 I felt *exhausted / exhausting* after running in such a long race.
6 I get *annoyed / annoying* with my little brother when he behaves like that.
7 Some of the awful things on the TV news make me feel a bit *depressing / depressed.*
8 'Stranger Things' is one of the most *excited / exciting* series on television.

👁 *B1 Preliminary* candidates often make mistakes with *–ed* and *–ing* adjectives.

3 **Some of these sentences are correct and some have mistakes. Correct the sentences that are wrong.**

1 I felt very tiring after doing homework all evening.
2 It was a very frightened book, but I read it all and I enjoyed it.
3 Thomas explained the rules of the game, but we were still a bit confused.
4 After a week at school, I just want to stay at home and feel relaxing.
5 There are some really excited rides at the summer fair.
6 I'm a bit worrying about my friend Lacey. She hasn't phoned.
7 Something really embarrassing happened to me yesterday.
8 I was very surprising when I saw that famous singer in our street.

FOCUS: IDENTIFYING KEY WORDS IN EXAM QUESTIONS

4 Look at these typical Part 3 questions and unfinished statements. Underline the key words in each.

1 What does the writer like most about playing the trumpet?

2 The writer felt nervous when he answered the phone because …

3 How did Emma feel about going to a new school?

4 Francesca was bored during the train journey because …

5 Why did the writer decide to get a new bike?

6 According to Liam, the main difference between badminton and tennis is …

FOCUS: ANSWERING MULTIPLE-CHOICE QUESTIONS IN YOUR OWN WORDS

5 Quickly read this paragraph and answer these questions.

1 What kind of text is it?

2 What's it about?

3 How does the speaker feel?

On my first day at the snowboarding school I was in a beginners group of twelve, although some were clearly 'advanced beginners'. Before the instructor arrived they started showing the rest of us the cool things they could do, which I think annoyed some in the group, though I didn't mind. I wanted to learn to snowboard well, and I felt sure that if I watched others, listened to the instructor and kept practising, I would, in the end, achieve that. Previously, I'd watched snowboarding competitions and I'd wondered whether it really could be as much as fun as it looked, and by the end of that week I was starting to find that it was. It was also a bit less tiring than I'd expected.

6 Look at this question, underline the key words and then read the paragraph above more carefully. Try to answer the question in your own words.

How did the writer feel when he first went snowboarding?

7 Now look at options A, B, C and D. Which best matches your own answer in Exercise 6? Check your answer. Why are the other options wrong?

A exhausted after doing so much hard exercise

B confident that he could become good at it

C disappointed that it was not an exciting sport to do

D angry with some of the learners in his group

TIP Try answering the question for yourself before looking at options A–D. Then choose the option that's closest to your own answer.

Questions 11–15

For each question, choose the correct answer.

Coasteering

Lily Carter had no idea what present she wanted for her 14th birthday. But she'd always been keen on challenging sports, especially to do with water, like surfing and sailing. So when her parents heard about an activity called coasteering – exploring rocks along the coast by climbing and swimming – they thought Lily would love it. They found a course offered at an activity centre called Porthdean, just along the coast from the family home, which was perfect. So after checking it was led by experienced instructors, they signed her up.

Lily had seen a TV show about coasteering, and was interested in doing it, although she'd thought only adults could take part. But then she discovered that on courses at Porthdean, there'd also be people her age jumping from rocks into the sea, and also exploring caves – which she was never normally allowed to do, so she really wanted to go. But she still asked her dad to go along too and, although he wondered whether he'd like coasteering himself, he knew how much Lily wanted someone to accompany her, so he agreed.

Lily and her dad drove to Porthdean, where they attended a session with their instructors to learn basic safety and techniques and be given helmets and special wetsuits to keep the cold out. The group they joined was quite small, which meant they got lots of individual attention. Says Lily, 'The entire trip was awesome – although the water was freezing! But our instructors encouraged the whole group so much, we were ready to try absolutely all the challenges, even stuff we hadn't expected at all, like jumping off high cliffs! I must admit, the one I jumped off wasn't that high, but Dad went much higher!'

'Anyway, Dad and I hadn't realised how hard it would be physically, so we were glad we were fit,' explains Lily. 'Even so, afterwards, we actually felt like we'd done loads of hard exercise in the gym! But I'll keep the memories of that trip forever, I reckon. And the instructors are going to put a video of it onto the website, so my friends will see it. They'd never believe me otherwise!'

11 Why did Lily's parents choose Porthdean for her coasteering present?

    A It offered various courses in her favourite watersport.

    B The instructors there were highly recommended.

    C It wasn't too far away from where they lived.

    D She had already tried some activities there.

12 How did Lily feel about the coasteering course?

    A pleased that it included something she'd always wanted to try

    B excited about doing the experience all on her own

    C keen to find out more about what it involved

    D interested to see whether she was the only teenager

13 Lily particularly liked her instructors because they made sure everyone

    A was comfortable with the kit they were given.

    B felt confident about the new things they would attempt.

    C got the same amount of attention.

    D knew all the activities they would take part in.

14 Lily says that after the course, she was

    A happy she'd shared something so exciting with her dad.

    B sorry she hadn't worked at getting fitter before she went.

    C proud that her friends all thought she'd done well.

    D surprised at how exhausted she was by the activities.

15 What would Lily text to a friend while she was away on the course?

A

> I don't think Dad was sure before he came that he'd enjoy it – but actually, he's been braver than me!

B

> I wanted to do the coasteering course, and mentioned it to my parents before my birthday. But I never expected they'd let me go!

C

> Our session before the activities was great, although I really didn't think I'd need a wetsuit for the cold – and I was right!

D

> Going into caves was amazing. I'd love to explore them by myself when we're next at the beach – I'm sure my parents will let me!

- How many gaps are there in the text?
- How many sentences must you choose from?

VOCABULARY: SYNONYMS

1 Match the common phrases in box A with their meanings in box B.

A	a lack of	get better	get in touch	hardly ever	in the end	make your mind up
	on your own	rather than	so far	take care of	take it easy	up-to-date

B	almost never	by yourself	contact	decide	finally	improve
	instead of	look after	modern	not enough	relax	until now

GRAMMAR: LINKING EXPRESSIONS

👁 *B1 Preliminary* candidates often make mistakes with expressions that link sentences.

2 Choose the correct word or phrase in these sentences.

1 We decided not to buy that car because it was too big. *Another / Other* reason was that it was too expensive.

2 It was the middle of the night. *Although / In spite of* that, the streets were crowded with people.

3 There was writing on the wall of the cave. *What / Which* it said was impossible to read.

4 The morning was sunny and hot. *So / However*, in the afternoon it became cold and wet.

5 Our plan was to get to the station early, but we missed the train. *Also / Instead*, we went by bus.

6 We'd better get some food. *Therefore / Otherwise*, we'll be hungry later.

FOCUS: USING SYNONYMS AND LINKING EXPRESSIONS AS CLUES

3 Match sentences 1–3 with sentences A–D to form a complete paragraph. There's one sentence which you don't need to use. Look for synonyms and linking expressions to help you.

1 Lucas was hoping to spend the morning taking it easy at home.

2 It was from Jake, who was walking in the countryside, and he sounded worried.

3 Jake replied that he was by himself in cold, thick fog and was completely lost.

A As soon as he heard that, Lucas knew he couldn't leave his friend out there on his own.

B That was why he was alone in the hills in winter.

C However, his plans for a relaxing Sunday ended when he received a phone call.

D So Lucas asked him what was wrong.

4 Work in pairs. Highlight the linking expressions, synonyms and reference words that help link each correct sentence A–D with 1–3. Which words tell you why one of them doesn't fit any of 1–3?

Questions 16–20

Five sentences have been removed from the text below. For each question, choose the correct answer.
There are three extra sentences which you do not need to use.

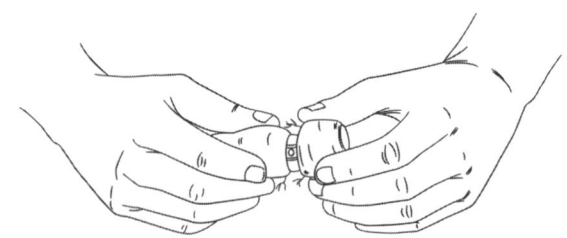

The story of the carrot and the ring

Have you ever lost something that was precious to you, and thought you'd never see it again? That's what happened to Mary Grams from Canada.

Mary had worn her engagement ring for more than half a century when she suddenly lost it. She was working in her garden on the family farm one day, pulling out a plant. **16**   When she discovered it was missing, she searched everywhere for it for days, before finally giving up.

Mary realised she probably wasn't going to find the ring again. So she decided not to tell anyone about what had happened, apart from her son. Instead, she thought she would replace it with a much cheaper ring from a jeweller's. **17**   In fact, it was so similar that no-one else in her family even knew her original ring was missing.

But the story has a happy ending. Mary eventually got her engagement ring back – 13 years after it was lost! One day Mary's daughter-in-law Colleen was working in the same garden where Mary had been all those years ago.

18   But this time it looked a bit different – because there was a carrot growing right through the middle of it!

As soon as Colleen saw the ring, she knew immediately who the owner was. The farm had been in the family for over 100 years. **19**   So when Colleen discovered the story of the lost ring, it became clear there was only one person it could possibly have belonged to, and the ring was returned to Mary.

Mary decided to remove her ring from the carrot and wear it again. **20**   Then the ring was washed, and Mary put it back on her finger – and it still fitted perfectly!

TIP   Check that the verb form and any singular or plural nouns all match in the main text and the sentence you have chosen.

A She was digging up vegetables there when she discovered the ring.

B That gave her a very good idea about what to do with the carrot.

C And that was probably when the ring came off her finger.

D So she carefully cut the carrot in half.

E She had never seen anything like it before.

F And only two women had lived there in all that time.

G It was tiring work, as some of them were very big.

H Luckily, she managed to find another one that looked just like it.

TIP After you choose all your answers, check that the completed text makes sense.

- How many gaps do you have to fill in?
- How many words do you choose from for each gap?

VOCABULARY: COLLOCATIONS

 B1 Preliminary candidates often make mistakes with verb/noun collocations.

1 Some words commonly go together. Match each word or phrase in the box with the verb *do*, *make*, *have* or *take*.

a bus	a noise	a job	a photo	sport	an exercise	an idea	a break	fun	a party
a good time	a mess	a mistake	a shower	a phone call	an exam		friends	an English course	
my homework	notes	a good time	lunch at school		school		some shopping		

2 Find and correct the mistakes in these sentences. Use verbs from Exercise 1.

1 I can't go out because I haven't made my homework yet.

2 We passed a really good time during our holidays.

3 My friend Marta is making a party on Saturday evening.

4 I'm feeling tired, so I'm going to do a short break.

5 I'm sure you'll soon know new friends when you change school.

6 The primary school kids were doing a lot of noise.

7 I want to learn Chinese, so I'm giving lessons every week.

8 Try not to do any mistakes in this exercise!

TIP It's very useful to learn common English verb+noun collocations.

FOCUS: USING COLLOCATIONS AS CLUES

3 Quickly read the text in Exercise 4 below, without looking at options A, B, C and D or filling in any gaps. What kind of text is it and what is it about?

4 Choose the best word, A, B, C or D, for each gap. Underline any words before or after the gap that often go with one of those options.

Last March my friends and I (1) .... some free time, so we decided to go abroad. We (2) .... a week in the wonderful city of Barcelona, seeing the sights, eating wonderful meals and (3) .... some great shopping! While we were there, we (4) .... the underground train and then a cable car right to the top of Montjuic Hill, where we (5) .... the most amazing views across the city.

1	A	did	B	had	C	made	D	went
2	A	passed	B	took	C	paid	D	spent
3	A	making	B	buying	C	doing	D	having
4	A	took	B	arrived	C	brought	D	travelled
5	A	saw	B	caught	C	got	D	gave

TIP For each gap, decide what kind of word, the 4 options are, e.g. noun, verb.

Questions 21–26

For each question, choose the correct answer.

Sheep can recognise faces!

Many people think sheep aren't very intelligent creatures. But in fact, **(21)** .... to new research, they may be cleverer than we think. For example, sheep can actually be trained to recognise human faces from photographs!

Recognising faces is an important human social **(22)** .... However, it seems that sheep are also social animals that can recognise other sheep as well as **(23)** .... humans. In experiments, researchers trained eight sheep to recognise the faces of celebrities from photographs. Training involved getting the sheep to **(24)** .... decisions about the photos they saw. At one end of a room, they would see two different photographs, and would receive a **(25)** .... of food for approaching the photograph of the celebrity; if they approached the wrong photograph, they got nothing. Over time, they learned to **(26)** .... getting food with the celebrity's photograph. And after training, the sheep correctly chose the celebrity's face eight times out of ten!

21	A	regarding	B	following	C	resulting	D according
22	A	skill	B	talent	C	knowledge	D method
23	A	ordinary	B	usual	C	familiar	D frequent
24	A	set	B	make	C	have	D do
25	A	reward	B	benefit	C	tip	D goal
26	A	attach	B	join	C	add	D connect

- How many gaps are there in the text?
- How many words must you write in each gap?

GRAMMAR: RELATIVE PRONOUNS

 *B1 Preliminary* candidates often make mistakes with relative pronouns.

1 **Correct the mistakes in these sentences using the relative pronouns in the box.**

> which   who   where   when   whose

1 The fish who I saw was a shark, I think.
2 Buenos Aires, which my cousins live, is a long way from here.
3 My big sister Layla, that is 17, is going to university next year.
4 The neighbours, which house is much bigger than ours, have two cars.
5 That's the boy which I told you about.
6 It was in February, where the weather was cold, that I bought this coat.
7 A good cook is someone who food always tastes good!
8 There's the house that I used to live.

> **TIP** For each gap, first decide what kind of word you need, e.g. a pronoun.

FOCUS: IDENTIFYING PART OF SPEECH

2 **Complete each sentence with one word.**

1 The girl .... lives in that house goes to my school.
2 In some countries you can't drive a car .... you're 18.
3 We'll go to the shopping mall tomorrow if we .... enough time.
4 Take some money with you in .... you want to buy a drink.
5 I always like to take part .... as many different sports as I can.
6 Let's leave now .... we don't have to run to catch the bus.

> **TIP** After you fill in all the gaps, make sure the completed text makes sense.

3 **Which of your answers above are:**

- verb forms? (e.g. *was*)
- prepositions? (e.g. *of*)
- linking words or part of linking expressions? (e.g. *though, in order to*)
- relative pronouns? (e.g. *which*)

4 **In pairs, look at the gaps in this paragraph and for each one decide what kind of word is needed. Then complete each gap with one suitable word.**

Snow biking is a new winter sport (1) .... is now becoming very popular. It's similar (2) .... mountain biking in that it involves riding down steep hills, often at high speed, but on snow or ice (3) .... of on ordinary ground. Snow biking tyres, (4) .... , have to be wider than those on a mountain bike, (5) .... that the wheels don't slip on icy surfaces.

Questions 27–32

For each question, write the correct word. Write **one** word for each gap.

Central College student fashion show – review

by Sam Coulston, college magazine reporter

As you may know, we had a fantastic fashion show here at the college last week. The aim was to display the work that the fashion students (27) .... recently been involved in all year here at the college, and show parents and friends the results. And it was clear to us that (28) .... were impressed by it.

The models that (29) .... part in the show were actually the students themselves, wearing their own clothes designs. (30) .... were some amazingly creative clothes on show, such as a dress made of recycled materials, and a coat that included every colour you could possibly think of! And the scenery, created (31) .... the students in the Art Department, was really spectacular too.

Mrs Jackson, Head of Design, said: 'There's absolutely (32) .... doubt in my mind that all these students are extremely talented – and I'm sure we'll hear more about them in the future. I wish them every success in their careers.'

- What do you have to read?
- How many points must you include in your email?

FOCUS: GIVING REASONS

1 **Choose the correct words.**

1 Lacey couldn't go to school *because / because of* her illness.

2 *As / Due to* heavy traffic in the city centre, our bus was late.

3 I'll take plenty of money *in case / because* I'm going to go shopping.

4 *As / Because of* we were feeling tired, we stopped for a break.

5 *Since / Due to* there's no school tomorrow, let's play tennis in the morning.

6 You'd better take a map with you *if / in case* you get lost.

◉ *B1 Preliminary* candidates often make mistakes with language for explaining the reason for something.

2 **Some of these sentences are correct and some have mistakes. Correct the sentences that are wrong.**

1 I'd love to visit your country as I believe it's really beautiful.

2 Why don't you reserve a table in the restaurant since it's full?

3 As the cold weather, we should wear warm clothes.

4 Since it'll be late when the film finishes, my parents will collect us from the cinema.

5 I'm afraid I can't come to your house on Sunday because of we'll be away then.

6 Shall we get to the cinema early, just in case it's really busy?

> **Remember**
>
> Put a noun after *because of* or *due to*, but a subject + verb after *because, as, since* or *in case*.

FOCUS: LANGUAGE TO BEGIN AND END AN EMAIL

3 **Decide if you would use each phrase at or near the *beginning* or *end* of an email. Then tick (✓) the phrases that you would use in an email to a friend.**

Dear Ms ...,
Write back soon.
Lots of love,
Thank you for your recent message.
Best wishes,
I look forward to hearing from you.

Hi ...,
See you soon.
Sorry I've taken so long to get back to you.
Yours sincerely,
It's great to hear from you!
Bye for now,

FOCUS: UNDERSTANDING THE TASK

4 **Read the exam instructions and the email on the opposite page, then answer questions 1–3.**

1 Who has written to you?

2 What is their email about?

3 What do the notes say you must do?

Read this email from your English-speaking friend Chris and the notes you have made. Write your answer in about 100 words. Write your **email** to Chris using **all the notes**.

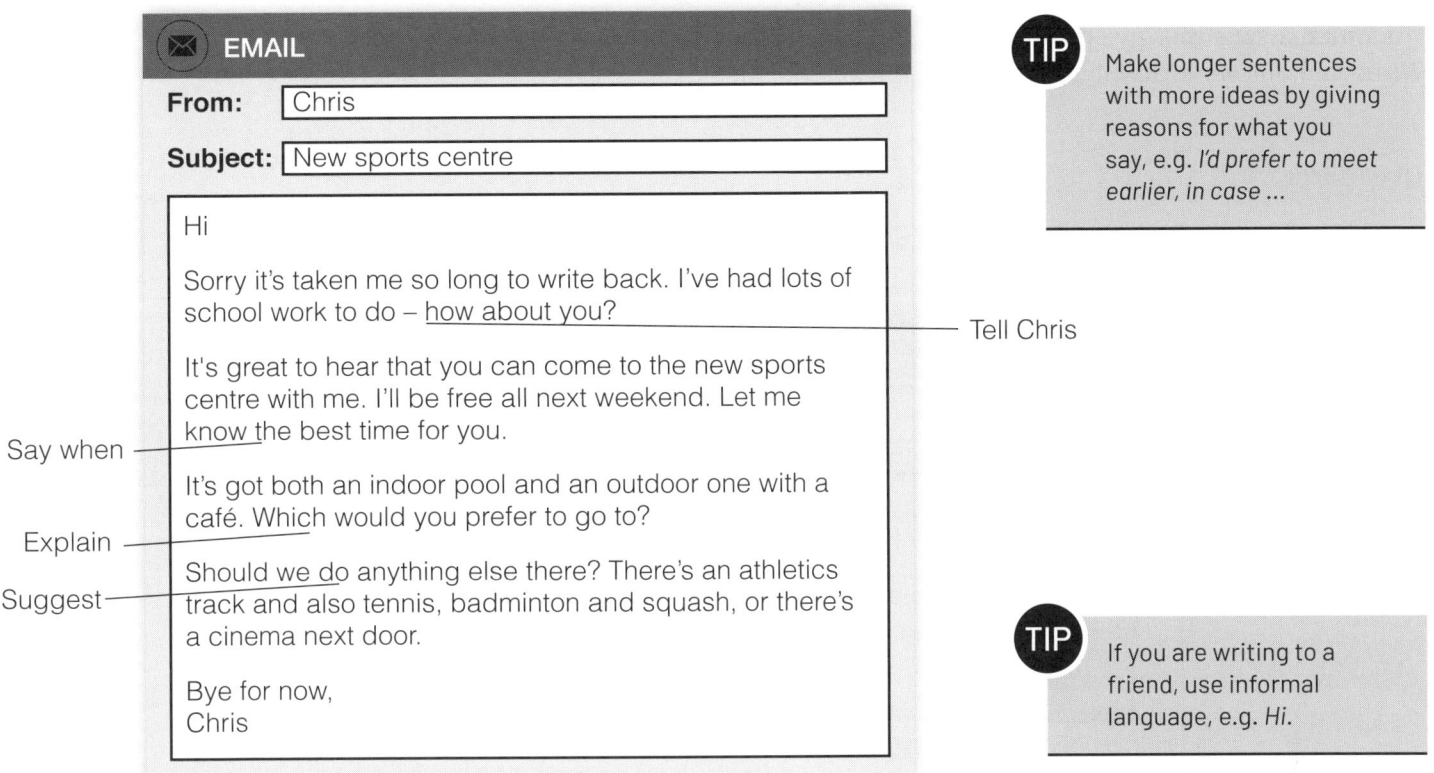

EMAIL

From: Chris

Subject: New sports centre

Hi

Sorry it's taken me so long to write back. I've had lots of school work to do – how about you? —————— Tell Chris

It's great to hear that you can come to the new sports centre with me. I'll be free all next weekend. Let me know the best time for you.

— Say when

It's got both an indoor pool and an outdoor one with a café. Which would you prefer to go to?

— Explain

Should we do anything else there? There's an athletics track and also tennis, badminton and squash, or there's a cinema next door.

— Suggest

Bye for now,
Chris

TIP Make longer sentences with more ideas by giving reasons for what you say, e.g. *I'd prefer to meet earlier, in case …*

TIP If you are writing to a friend, use informal language, e.g. *Hi*.

5 Does the writer of the email use formal or informal language? Find examples.

FOCUS: STUDYING A SAMPLE ANSWER

6 In pairs, read this sample reply to Chris and answer the questions.

> Hi Chris,
> Don't worry about taking your time replying. I've been really busy with exam revision!
>
> Going to the sports centre is a brilliant idea, as I really need to get fit. How about meeting there early on Saturday morning?
>
> I think I'd rather swim in the outdoor pool, in case we get hungry and feel like having something to eat. Maybe we could try the indoor one in the winter?
>
> I've always wanted to try squash, because it's so fast and it looks like really good exercise. Shall we book a court?
>
> Looking forward to hearing from you.
> All the best,
> Harper

1 Is it the right length?
2 Does it cover all four notes? In which paragraphs?
3 Is it written in formal or informal language? Find examples.
4 Which reason links (e.g. *since*) does the writer use?

You **must** answer this question.
Write your answer in about **100 words** on the answer sheet.

Question 1

Read this email from your English teacher and the notes you have made.

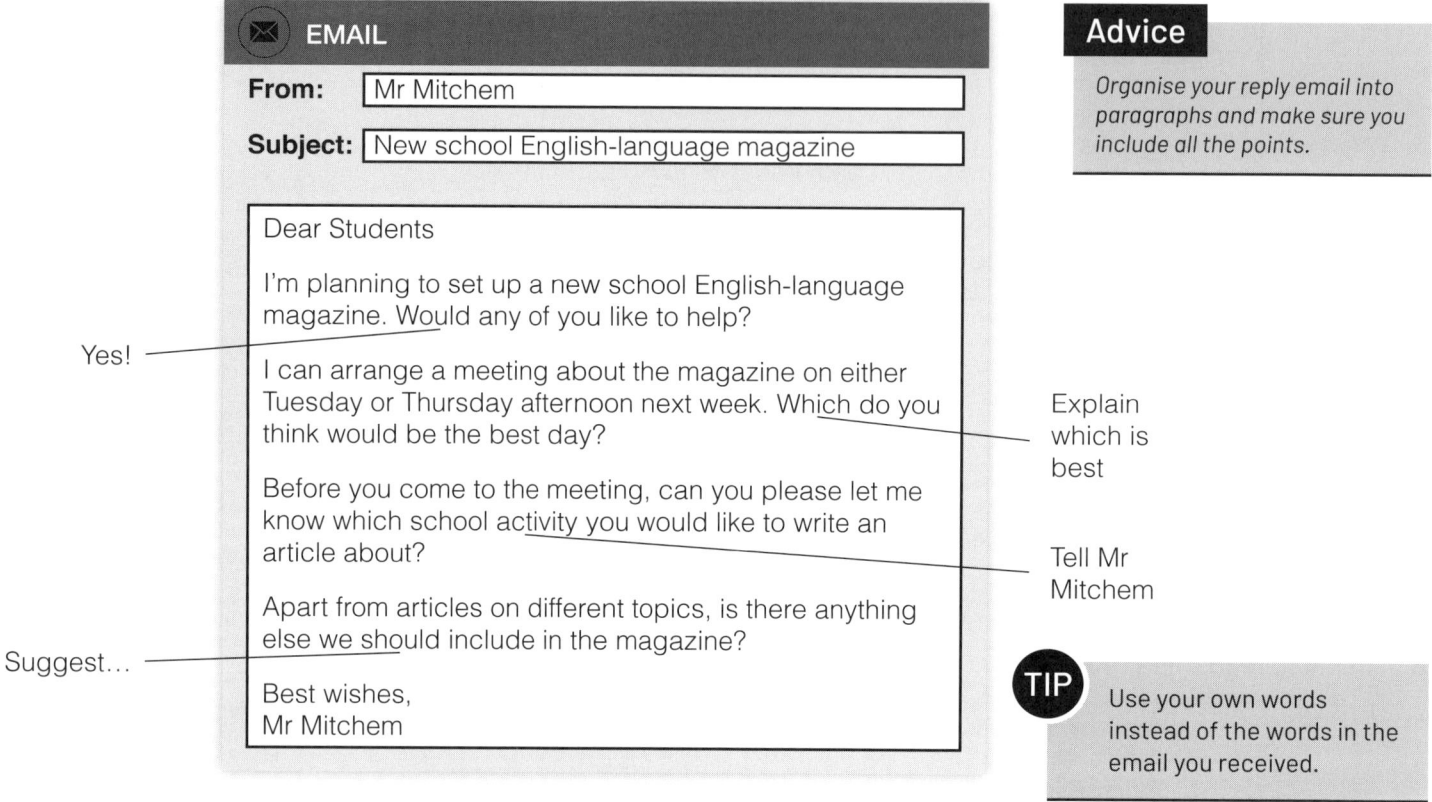

EMAIL

From: Mr Mitchem

Subject: New school English-language magazine

Dear Students

I'm planning to set up a new school English-language magazine. Would any of you like to help? — Yes!

I can arrange a meeting about the magazine on either Tuesday or Thursday afternoon next week. Which do you think would be the best day? — Explain which is best

Before you come to the meeting, can you please let me know which school activity you would like to write an article about? — Tell Mr Mitchem

Apart from articles on different topics, is there anything else we should include in the magazine? — Suggest...

Best wishes,
Mr Mitchem

Advice

Organise your reply email into paragraphs and make sure you include all the points.

TIP Use your own words instead of the words in the email you received.

Write your **email** to Mr Mitchem using **all the notes**.

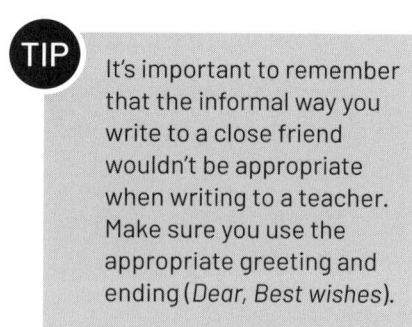

TIP It's important to remember that the informal way you write to a close friend wouldn't be appropriate when writing to a teacher. Make sure you use the appropriate greeting and ending (*Dear, Best wishes*).

- Do you write one or two texts in Part 2?
- What kinds of text will you write?

GRAMMAR: PAST TENSES

 B1 Preliminary candidates often make mistakes when using past tenses.

1 Match the sentences to their descriptions.

1 I went there last Saturday.
2 She was playing volleyball all day.
3 After he had watched the film he went outside.

a Something that was happening in the past.
b A past event which happened before another past event.
c A single event in the past.

2 Complete the sentence with the past simple or past continuous form of the verb in brackets.

1 He .... an apple when the teacher .... into the classroom. (eat, come)
2 Do you know what Henry .... all evening? There was a lot of noise! (do)
3 My mum .... when she saw my exam result. (smile)
4 My brother .... a glass while he .... the washing up. (break, do)
5 Joe .... until 10 o'clock yesterday morning. (not wake up)
6 We .... to the cinema last weekend and we .... a great film. (go, see)
7 I .... a police car while I .... home from school. (saw, walk)
8 Dad .... me to school this morning because I .... late. (drive, be)

3 Circle the correct tense in each sentence.

1 After I *was going / went* outside, I *realised / was realising* that I *forgot / had forgotten* my keys.
2 Clare *was standing / stood* at the bus stop when Martin *arrived / had arrived* there.
3 After I *had eaten / was eating* all the chips, mum *told / had told* me they were for my dad.
4 Sue *had spent / was spending* all morning in the park before she *had come / came* to my house.
5 My brother *played / had played* football yesterday until it *started / was starting* to rain.
6 While Tom *was waiting / had waited* at the station, he *saw / had seen* a poster for a band that he *hadn't heard / didn't hear* before.

4 Complete the story with the correct past tense of these verbs.

watch	look	~~get~~	happen	start
decide	be	begin	lose	tell	sit

By the time I (0) ..*got*.. to the cinema, the film (1) ....
My friends (2)................... at the back of the cinema and (3)
they .... the film. I asked them what (4) .... at
the beginning of the film, but as soon as they (5) .... to
explain, other people (6) .... at them to be quiet!
After the film, we (7) .... to go to a café to get an ice-
cream. I (8) .... for my phone to call my parents, but it
(9) .... in my pocket. I (10) .... it!

FOCUS: UNDERSTANDING THE TASK

5 Look at the exam task below and answer these questions.

1 What must you write?

2 Who is your reader?

3 What must you include in your answer? Where?

> **Write your answer in about 100 words on the answer sheet.**
>
> Your English teacher has asked you to write a story.
>
> Your story must begin with this sentence:
>
> *Before I could answer my phone, it stopped ringing.*
>
> Write your **story.**

FOCUS: STUDYING A SAMPLE ANSWER

6 Read this sample answer to the exam question above and answer questions 1–4.

1 Does the answer include the sentence given?

2 Is it the right length?

3 Does it describe how the character feels?

4 Does it have a happy or a sad ending?

TIP You must use the sentence given at the beginning of the story.

> Before I could answer my phone, it stopped ringing. I was riding along a busy road and by the time I was able to stop safely, I'd missed the call. I didn't recognise the number and when I rang back it was engaged, so I wondered who'd called me. Had something happened at home? Was my school trying to contact me, and if so, why? Worried, I got back on my bike. As soon as I was moving, my phone rang again and I answered just in time. A friendly voice told me I'd won a prize in a writing competition I'd entered a month earlier. I was delighted!

TIP Describe how the main character feels during the story.

TIP Try to connect your ideas so your sentences are not too short. In stories use time links, e.g. *after* ... .

7 Look at the sample answer more carefully and answer these questions.

1 What time links does the writer use? e.g. *Before...*

2 Find examples of the past simple, the past continuous and the past perfect.

Choose **one** of these questions.
Write your answer in about **100 words** on the answer sheet.

··

Question 2

You see this notice on an international English website for young people.

> **Articles wanted!**
>
> **PLAYING GAMES**
>
> Write an article telling us which kind of games you think are more interesting to play: board games or video games.
>
> What can people learn from playing games?
>
> The best article answering these questions will be published next month.

Advice

*Underline some of the key language in the notice to help guide you when you write the article. The article is asking for your opinion about a particular topic, so you can write the article in the first person (**In my opinion, I believe, I think**, etc.)*

Write your **article**.

Question 3

Your English teacher has asked you to write a story. Your story must begin with this sentence:

The friends found a strange old map under the bed.

Write your **story**.

TIP

Before you start writing, note down any key vocabulary related to the topic of the story. If you can use unusual words, a range of adjectives, adverbs and tenses, then your story will be more interesting and you will get better marks.

Marlon **Zoe** **Kam**

- How many questions are in Part 1?
- Will you listen to one long recording or several shorter recordings?

VOCABULARY: PERSONAL APPEARANCE

1 For each phrase below, write M (Marlon), Z (Zoe) or K (Kam).

This person ....

1 .... is wearing glasses.
2 .... has straight, dark hair.
3 .... has a moustache.
4 .... has long, blond hair.

5 .... has trainers on.
6 .... is bald.
7 .... is casually dressed.
8 .... is smartly dressed and has a beard.

9 .... has curly hair.
10 .... is wearing high heels.
11 .... is wearing a dress.
12 .... is wearing a suit.

2 Listen to someone describe Kam. There is one mistake. Can you find it?

3 Match the weather expressions to the symbols.

1 It's sunny.
2 The wind is very strong.
3 It's raining heavily.
4 There's a lot of ice and snow around.
5 It's cloudy.
6 There may be thunderstorms later.
7 It's foggy.

a  e

b f

c g

d

4 Look at the pictures and describe the weather in each one.

A B C

Listen and decide which picture shows the weather in

1 Scotland. 2 Northern England. 3 Wales.

FOCUS: IDENTIFYING WRONG INFORMATION

5 Complete the text with words from the box.

usually	thought	sure	instead	for a change
in the end	actually	although	should	tried

1 I .... the test was on Thursday, but it was .... on Friday.

2 I was .... Maria had made the poster, but I found out it was Rachel.

3 I .... eat sandwiches for lunch, but today I had pasta ....

4 He went to every shop to find a purple tie, but .... he bought a blue one.

5 .... I had tickets for the music festival, I was ill so I had to stay at home ....

6 The flight .... have left at 7.15, but it was delayed.

7 I .... to get a discount, but I had to pay the full price.

6 Which word is used in all the sentences in Exercise 5 except number 5? Which word with a similar meaning is used in sentence 5?

7 Listen and choose the correct picture. What did the girl buy?

A

B

C

Listen again. Which words helped you decide which answers are wrong?

PRONUNCIATION: WEAK FORMS

8 Listen and write the number of words in each sentence.

1 .... 2 .... 3 ....

4 .... 5 .... 6 ....

TIP Some words and phrases are frequently used to introduce a change in the speaker's original idea or preference. Listening for that language will help you identify incorrect answers.

TIP Some words are pronounced 'weakly' in sentences. That means we can't always hear them clearly.

Questions 1–7

28 For each question, choose the correct answer.

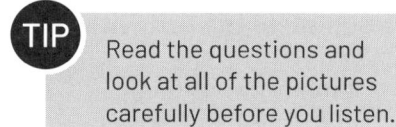
1 Where did the boy find his mobile phone?

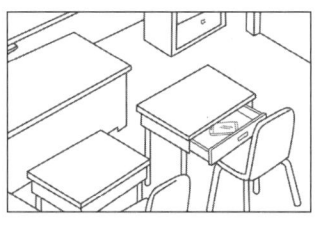

A

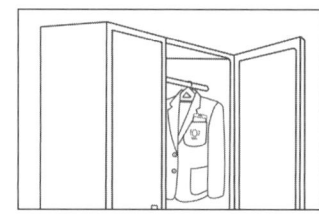

B

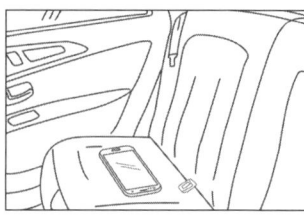

C

2 Which programme does the girl want to watch?

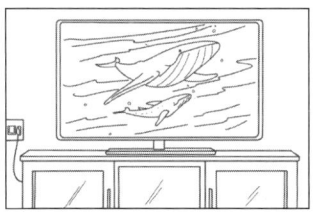

A

B

C

3 Which animals did the girl enjoy seeing the most?

A

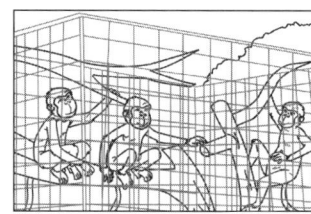

B

C

4 What will the boy look like in his school play?

A   B   C

5 What's the weather going to be like tomorrow?

A   B   C

6 Where does the girl want to meet her friend?

A   B   C

7 How much did the book cost?

A   B   C

- How many questions are there in this part?
- What type of questions are they?

FOCUS: UNDERSTANDING THE SPEAKER'S ATTITUDE

1 **Listen to the speakers. Choose the correct option.**

1 The speaker *likes / doesn't like* this curry.

2 The speaker is *happy / unhappy* about the trip to Rome.

3 The speaker is *busy / relaxed*.

4 The speaker *has / hasn't* studied the heart.

5 The person the speaker was calling took a *long / short* time to answer.

VOCABULARY: *LIKE / BE LIKE / LOOK LIKE*

 B1 Preliminary candidates often make mistakes with the different meanings and uses of *like*.

2 **Match each question to two possible answers.**

1 What does Charles like?

2 What is Charles like?

3 What does Charles look like?

a He's average build with white hair.

b He's a really nice guy.

c Reading and going to the cinema.

d He looks a bit like me!

e He's very clever.

f Healthy things, such as fruit and salad.

3 **Listen to the conversation and answer the questions.**

1 What question with 'like' does the boy ask?

2 What does the girl say about the teacher?

    a She is strict but fair.

    b She is too strict.

    c She is not strict enough.

PRONUNCIATION: INTONATION

4 **Listen to the sentences. How do you think the speaker feels?**

1 keen / bored

2 unsure / excited

3 angry / sorry

4 worried / pleased

5 surprised / bored

 TIP Speakers do not always say what they mean directly. Adverbs, adjectives and *too / enough* can all be used to show how the speaker feels about something.

Remember

What does he like? means 'tell me what he enjoys'.
What is he like? means 'tell me what kind of person he is'.
What does he look like? means 'tell me about his physical appearance'.

 TIP Make sure you know the difference between questions with *like*, as it will help you to predict what the speaker will answer.

🎧 **Questions 8–13**

32 For each question, choose the correct answer.

8 You will hear two friends talking about a music performance.
The friends agree that
A the concert hall was too big.
B the performance was too short.
C the musicians needed more practice.

9 You will hear two friends talking about a play they have seen recently.
What surprised the girl about the play?
A how young the audience was
B how unusual the ending was
C how good the acting was

10 You will hear a boy telling a friend about an art course he went on.
What did the boy enjoy most about it?
A the strong focus on drawing and painting
B the teacher's sense of humour
C the variety of practice activities

11 You will hear two friends talking about getting to school.
The girl thinks that walking to school with her friends
A is a good way to be sociable.
B takes longer than walking alone.
C causes problems for other pedestrians.

12 You will hear a boy talking to a friend about his new house.
How does the boy feel about it?
A pleased with its location
B amazed at how big it is
C satisfied with how it's decorated

13 You will hear a girl talking about a day out with her family.
Why did the girl's family choose to go to the river?
A There are many things to do.
B It's close to where they live.
C It's a good place for a picnic.

- How many speakers do you hear in this part?
- Do you fill in gaps or choose from several options?

FOCUS: PREDICTING ANSWERS AND IGNORING UNNECESSARY INFORMATION

1 You are going to listen to Karim talking to other students about his work experience. Look at the gaps you need to fill and, with a partner, discuss the kind of information you will need for each gap. Then listen and complete the exercise. Write no more than two words.

33

Work experience at Butterfly World

Work starts at **(1)** ....
You should wear **(2)** ....
Don't bring **(3)** ....
My favourite part of the work experience was **(4)** .... the butterflies.
You should apply to work at Butterfly World by: **(5)** ....
Send your application by email to: Monica **(6)** ....

2 The recording will often include extra information that sounds right, but is not. You need to pick out the *right* information. Listen again and note down some examples of 'false answers'.

33

3 Now look at the notes in the Exam Practice section (questions 14–19). Answer the questions.
  1 Which gap needs a date?
  2 In which question do you think the answer will be spelt out?
  3 Which gap needs a job title?

FOCUS: UNDERSTANDING NUMBERS AND DATES

4 Listen and write the date, number or price you hear.

34

1 ....   2 ....   3 ....   4 ....
5 ....   6 ....   7 ....

TIP You can write dates using numbers, e.g. 17th August instead of seventeenth of August. It would also be OK to write 17.8 or 8.17.

Questions 14–19

35

For each question, write the correct answer in the gap.
Write **one** or **two words** or a **number** or a **date** or a **time**.

You will hear a teacher giving some information about a school photography competition.

School photography competition

The subject of this year's competition is **(14)** ....

Photos must show some **(15)** ....

A local **(16)** .... will judge the competition.

First prize is a photography **(17)** ....

Send your entries in by **(18)** .... at the latest.

School secretary's email address is **(19) k.** .... **@school.com**

TIP Spelling questions are common in Part 3, so practise spelling out names and writing them down with a partner before the exam.

- How many speakers are there in Part 4?
- Will you hear facts, opinions or both?

VOCABULARY: COMPUTERS

1   Complete the sentences with a computer-related word from the box.

delete	podcasts	selfies	password	connection
laptop	install	app	social media	hardware

1   It's easy to make friends on ....

2   You can't access your email without a ....

3   .... means things like printers and keyboards – things you can touch.

4   My sister takes lots of .... She loves the way she looks.

5   After you download the software, you need to .... it on your computer.

6   Do you prefer working on a PC or a ....?

7   Make sure you don't .... my homework!

8   Listening to .... on different topics will help you improve your English.

9   How is the internet .... at your place?

10   I use a dictionary .... to check words I don't know.

VOCABULARY: OPPOSITE MEANINGS

2   Complete the sentences with an antonym of the underlined adjective.

1   Do you live <u>close</u> to the school?
Yes, not very .... away.

2   That lesson was so <u>boring</u>, wasn't it?
It wasn't very ...., was it?

3   Do you have much <u>free</u> time at the moment?
Well, I'm not very ....

4   Your bicycle is so <u>dirty</u>!
I know. It's not very ...., is it?

5   That hamburger was <u>disgusting</u>!
You're right. It wasn't very ....

6   Mr Johnson looks <u>sad</u>.
He doesn't look very ...., does he?

> **Remember**
>
> Instead of saying something is *bad*, some speakers might use the antonym *good* after *not very*.

FOCUS: PARAPHRASE

3   Match the extracts from the Exam Practice recording with a paraphrase.

1   I certainly don't have many opportunities to get bored.

2   I couldn't believe how well it worked.

3   I learn better by doing than by studying.

4   There are hundreds of websites about this too.

5   I was wondering about possible solutions to this.

a   I was surprised that it was so successful.

b   Studying is not as useful for me as experience.

c   My life is very rarely dull.

d   I thought about how we could solve this problem.

e   Many sites deal with that as well.

Questions 20–25

36   For each question, choose the correct answer.

You will hear an interview with a 15-year-old boy called Callum, who runs a successful book review website for teenagers.

20   How did Callum learn about setting up a website?
- **A**   through lessons at school
- **B**   by using information online
- **C**   a family member taught him

21   Why did Callum decide to set up a book review website?
- **A**   to develop teenagers' writing skills
- **B**   to encourage teenagers to read more
- **C**   to create an online discussion among teenagers

22   How did Callum feel when his site first went online?
- **A**   pleased with its quality
- **B**   certain it would be popular
- **C**   positive it would achieve its aims

23   What does Callum say about a typical day?
- **A**   It's usually full of variety.
- **B**   It's always extremely busy.
- **C**   It's impossible to predict what will happen.

24   When Callum is eighteen he'd like to
- **A**   work for a big company.
- **B**   study for a degree.
- **C**   run a business.

25   What is Callum's new website for?
- **A**   using music to help people
- **B**   presenting new music
- **C**   learning how to play music

TIP   The questions often use different words from the recording, so listen for words and phrases that say the same thing in a different way.

TIP   Questions about feelings are common in Part 4. You need to listen for the feeling, e.g. *certain*, with the reason or result, e.g. *it would be popular*.

TIP Make sure you can say how old you are, where you live and who you live with. Everyone is asked these questions.

- Who do you have to talk to in Part 1 of the test?
- What do you have to do in this part of the test?
- How long do you have to talk for?

1 Complete the sentences about the people who are involved in the speaking test.

> assessor   interlocutor   candidates

1 The .... is the person who asks the questions.

2 The .... doesn't speak during the test, but listens and gives the marks.

3 The .... are the people who are taking the test.

FOCUS: COMMON QUESTIONS

2 Put these common Part 1 Phase 2 questions into the correct order, then ask and answer them with a partner.

1 time / your / What / you / in / do / free / do ?

2 English / did / When / learning / you / start ?

3 favourite / your / us / teacher / about / Tell .

4 going / weekend / are / next / do / What / you / to ?

5 dinner / do / usually / you / What / for / eat ?

6 your / us / Tell / school / about .

7 doing / you / family / do / What / with / enjoy / your ?

8 go / do / usually / you / shopping / Where ?

TIP Try to avoid giving very short answers to Phase 2 questions like these. Give examples or talk about your experiences if you can.

3 Listen to an interlocutor asking a candidate called Juan the questions from Exercise 2. Correct the mistakes in the information.

🎧 37

1 Juan's favourite free time activity is watching TV.

2 Juan started learning English when he was four.

3 Juan's favourite teacher is his English teacher.

4 Juan is going to his cousin's house next weekend.

5 Juan usually has chicken for dinner.

6 Juan's school is very big.

7 Juan enjoys going out for walks with his family.

8 Juan usually goes shopping near his house.

4 Practise asking and answering the questions from Exercise 2 with a partner. Try and make your answers longer than Juan's answers.

TIP Listen carefully to your partner's answers to the questions. This may help you.

(2–3 minutes)

Phase 1
Interlocutor

To A/B   Good morning / afternoon / evening.
Can I have your mark sheets, please?
(Hand over the mark sheets to the assessor.)

To A/B   I'm .... and this is ....

To A   What's your name? How old are you?
Thank you.

To B   And what's your name? How old are you?
Thank you.

To B   B, where do you live?
Who do you live with?
Thank you.

To A   And A, where do you live?
Who do you live with?
Thank you.

> **TIP**   Listen to how your partner answers the questions. This may help you too.

Phase 2
Interlocutor

(The interlocutor may ask one or more of the following questions.)

Tell us about your home.

What do you use the internet for?

What do you usually do when you get home from school? (Why?)

What is your favourite day of the week? (Why?)

Would you like to learn to play a musical instrument? (Why? / Why not?)

How do you usually travel to school? (Why?)

What's your favourite kind of film? (Why?)

Tell us about the clothes you like wearing.

> **Advice**
>
> *Before the test, practise describing your daily life, your interests and your school life with a partner.*

- What will you be given to talk about in Part 2?
- How long do you have to talk for?

 When describing things, students sometimes make errors using *there is* and *there are*. Native speakers naturally use these structures more than others, but it's good to use a variety, such as *I can see …* .

FOCUS: DESCRIBING PHOTOGRAPHS

1 Work in pairs and each choose one of the photographs below (see colour version on page C10). Take it in turns to tell your partner what you can see in your photograph. Keep talking for one minute if you can.

2 Give your partner some feedback on how they did. Say what they did well and how they could improve their description.

3 Look at your photograph again. Describe it to your partner in more detail. Think about:

- who the people are
- where they are
- what they are doing
- why they are doing this
- what the weather is like
- what the people are wearing
- what you can see in the background.

4 Give your partner feedback on how they did. Say what they did well and how they could improve their description. Was it better than their first attempt?

5 Listen to a student describing one of the photos above. Which photo is he describing? Does he say the same things you said about the photo? What did he do well and how could he improve?

38

6 Listen to a student describing the other photo. Answer the questions in Exercise 5.

39

> **Remember**
>
> Use *there is …* to talk about singular and uncountable nouns, e.g. *There's a yellow school bus …*, and *there are …* to talk about plural nouns, e.g. *There are several children getting on the bus.*

> **TIP**
>
> If you don't know the word for something in the photograph, don't worry! Describe it using words that you do know, e.g. the colours, what it's used for.

> **Remember**
>
> Use phrases like these to say where things are.
> - *In the middle of the photo, there is …*
> - *On the back of the chair, there is …*
> - *Behind the students, there are …*
> - *On the shelves, there are …*
> Can you think of any more?

(3–5 minutes)

Interlocutor

> Now I'd like each of you to talk on your own about something. I'm going to give each of you a photograph and I'd like you to talk about it.
>
> **A**, here is your photograph. It shows some people **doing sport**.

The interlocutor will place Exam Practice Test 2 Speaking Part 2 picture (see page C1) in front of Candidate A.

> **B**, you just listen.
>
> **A**, please tell us what you can see in the photograph.

Candidate A

(Approximately 1 minute)

Interlocutor

> Thank you.

Back-up prompts (for A and B)
- Talk about the person/people.
- Talk about the place.
- Talk about other things in the photograph.

Interlocutor

> **B**, here is your photograph. It shows some people **helping at home**.

The interlocutor will place Exam Practice Test 2 Speaking Part 2 picture (see page C2) in front of Candidate B.

> **A**, you just listen.
>
> **B**, please tell us what you can see in the photograph.

Candidate B

(Approximately 1 minute)

Interlocutor

> Thank you.

Advice

When you're describing what the people are doing or what they're wearing, remember to use the present continuous tense: They are playing basketball, they are wearing shorts and T-shirts.

- Who will you talk with in Part 3?
- What will you be given to talk about?
- How long do you have to talk for?

Remember

There are lots of phrases you can use for asking for someone's opinion: *What do you think?... Do you agree?... What about you?... And you?*

FOCUS: GIVING OPINIONS AND ASKING FOR OPINIONS

1 **In Part 3, you have to discuss a situation with your partner.**

To do this, you'll need to use phrases for giving and asking for opinions. Complete the phrases with the words in the box. Use each word only once.

sure	agree	would	about	idea
what	think	opinion	prefer	best

1 I .... that having a meal together …

2 What .... you?

3 The .... thing to do is …

4 Do you ....?

5 .... do you think?

6 In my ...., they should …

7 I'm not so .... they should …

8 Is having a meal together a good ....?

9 Having a meal together .... be good.

10 I'd .... to go for a meal together.

2 **Listen to Angelika and Rafael talking about this situation: A photography teacher wants to organise an activity for her new students to get to know one another at the start of the course. The options Angelika and Rafael are discussing are in the box.**

🎧 40

Complete the conversation.

- going to the cinema together
- having a meal together
- photographing birds and animals together in the countryside
- playing a sport together, for example basketball

A: So **(1)** .... the teacher should do, Rafael?

R: Hmm … I think that photographing birds and animals **(2)** .... I mean, they're starting a photography course, so it **(3)** .... to do some photography together.

A: I'm **(4)** .... They'll be doing that a lot on the course, so **(5)** .... it'd be better to do something different, like going to the cinema.

R: But **(6)** .... it'd be very difficult to talk to each other at the cinema?

A: Oh yes, **(7)** ....! And not everyone likes sport, so **(8)** .... avoid that one.

R: **(9)** ...., but having a meal together is very sociable and a nice thing to do.

A: Yes, that's definitely **(10)** .... idea.

👁 This part of the test always includes a superlative (*the most interesting*, *the most fun*, *the best*), which students often make mistakes with. Remember to use *the most* before long adjectives like *interesting* and *useful*. Note that *the best* is irregular.

3 Talk with your partner about this situation: A teacher has asked her class what the most interesting way to learn about history would be.

Discuss these four options with your partner:

- visiting historic buildings
- watching historical dramas
- acting together to create a historical play
- reading historical stories together in class

Exam Practice Test 2   Speaking Part 3

(4–5 minutes)

TIP It's not a problem if you don't have time to talk about all of the pictures – you don't lose any marks.

Interlocutor	Now, in this part of the test you're going to talk about something together for about two minutes. I'm going to describe a situation to you.

The interlocutor will place the Exam Practice Test 2 Speaking Part 3 set of pictures (see page C12) in front of both candidates.

Interlocutor	**A teacher wants his class to learn more about space.** **Here are some different ways to learn about space.** **Talk together about the different ways to learn about space, and say which students would find most interesting.** All right? Now, talk together.

(Approximately 2–3 minutes)

Interlocutor	Thank you.

TIP Remember to work together to talk about the pictures and the task. You can ask each other questions, agree, disagree, take it in turns to talk about the pictures – it's up to you!

- Who will you talk to in this part of the test?
- What will you talk about?
- How long will you talk for?

TIP Try to share the speaking during a discussion. Don't talk all of the time or let your partner do all of the talking.

FOCUS: QUESTION FORMS

1 Match the question beginnings and endings below.

1	How often do you	a	with your friends online?
2	Where do you	b	with friends or with family?
3	Do you ever chat	c	about with your friends?
4	Do you have friends	d	playing games with friends?
5	What do you talk	e	best friend?
6	Do you like	f	meet with your friends?
7	Do you prefer to go out	g	who live in other countries?
8	Who's your	h	do you do together?
9	What kind of things	i	go together?

Remember

You can use words and phrases like these to give reasons for your opinions:
I think / don't think / prefer ... because ...
In my opinion, they should ... because ...
And these to justify your opinions:
People like ... so it's a good idea to ...
They can ... so that's why it's a good idea.

2 Now ask and answer the questions in Exercise 1 with a partner.

3 Look at the questions. Write down reasons for your answers, then ask and answer the questions with a partner, giving your reasons. Respond to what your partner says by agreeing or disagreeing, and giving opinions of your own, with a reason.

> Do you like doing homework with your friends?

> No, not really.

> Why not?

> Because we usually end up chatting rather than working, so it takes much longer to do it.

1 Do you like going out to eat with friends? Why? / Why not?
2 Do you prefer visiting friends at their homes or when friends come to your home? Why?
3 Do you think it's important to see your friends every day? Why? / Why not?
4 Is it important for good friends to have the same interests? Why? / Why not?

4 Listen to two students discussing what they talk to their friends about. Do they just give information or do they give reasons for their opinions? How could they improve their answers?

41

5 Now talk together about the best way to make new friends. Give reasons for your answers.

Exam Practice Test 2 — Speaking Part 4

(3–4 minutes)

Interlocutor
(to both candidates)

- Do you like learning about space? (Why? / Why not?)
- Would you like to travel to space one day? (Why? / Why not?)
- Do you think people will live on other planets one day? (Why? / Why not?)
- Do you like watching science fiction films that take place in space? (Why? / Why not?)
- Is it better to learn more about the Earth or more about space? (Why?)

Thank you. That is the end of the test.

Advice

Give some reasons for your answers. Examples (for *Would you like to travel to space one day?*):

Yes: *I'd be very excited to have that opportunity. I'd love to be able to see the Earth from space. I also think it would be amazing to float around in space just like an astronaut.*

No: *In my opinion, it would be too dangerous because a rocket has to travel at a very fast speed to reach space. Also, I might feel sick and you can't get off a spaceship!*

Can you think of any more reasons?

 TIP It is normal to make some mistakes during the test. Don't let these mistakes worry you – just continue with the test.

Test 3 · Reading Part 1

Questions 1–5

For each question, choose the correct answer.

1

Toni's Pizza Bar
Want to enjoy a pizza
with your friends?
This week only – special
offers on our giant pizzas.

A Choose which size of pizza you buy and still get a special price.

B Pay less at the moment for pizzas big enough to share with other people.

C The very big pizzas at Toni's are only available this week.

2

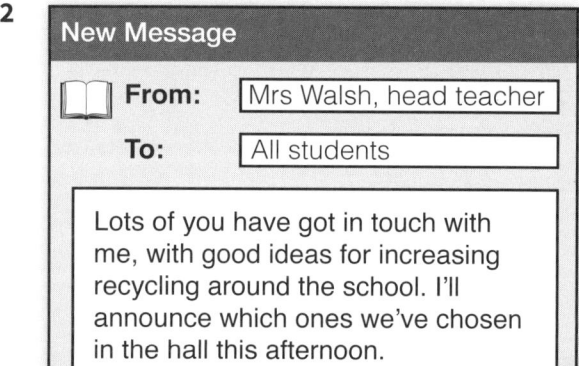

New Message

From: Mrs Walsh, head teacher

To: All students

Lots of you have got in touch with me, with good ideas for increasing recycling around the school. I'll announce which ones we've chosen in the hall this afternoon.

A Mrs Walsh wants students to contact her with plans for recycling around the school.

B Mrs Walsh intends to let students know which of their suggestions the school will use.

C Mrs Walsh wants students to go to the hall today to help recycle rubbish.

3

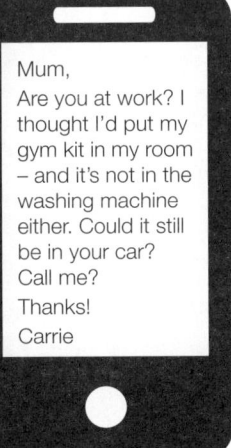

Tim
I'm going to a tree-planting day tomorrow, to help the environment by increasing the number of trees. If you're interested, come along – and bring some friends, if they'd also like to help!
Sarah

A   Sarah is keen to get others involved in an environmental project she's joining.

B   Sarah says a tree-planting project is still short of volunteers to complete their work.

C   Sarah is wondering whether to take part in a project with her friend.

4

BROWN'S BOOKS
Everything must go!
Moving to a new location in town
All goods, including books,
half-price this week.

A   This bookstore will no longer serve customers in the town after this week.

B   Only books are available here this week, at a reduced price.

C   To buy books from Brown's, find their new store in town after this week.

5

Mum,
Are you at work? I thought I'd put my gym kit in my room – and it's not in the washing machine either. Could it still be in your car? Call me?
Thanks!
Carrie

A   Carrie is asking if her mum has washed her gym kit for her.

B   Carrie has just remembered where she left her gym kit.

C   Carrie wonders if her mum has driven to work with her gym kit.

Questions 6–10

For each question, choose the correct answer.

The people below all want to watch an animated film.
On the opposite page there are reviews of eight animated films.
Decide which film would be the most suitable for the people below.

6 Kerim wants a film that uses traditional animation methods, such as simple drawings rather than computers to create pictures. He particularly enjoys films about animals, and with great songs sung by well-known singers.

7 Alice, her mum and small sister want a film they can all enjoy. Alice loves films where she feels the main characters are like her, and that have soundtracks involving only instruments, with no singing.

8 Lukas enjoys films that make him laugh, but that he can learn something from at the same time. He's a keen reader, and he'd like a film of something he's probably already read.

9 Minnie wants to see a happy film that isn't just about heroes against bad people. She'd like a film that's full of surprises, that she'll want to watch over and over again.

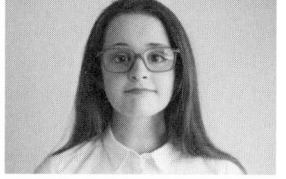

10 Susana wants to see a film about characters that show courage in different situations, and that have the voices of famous actors. She'd like the film to have really beautiful animation.

Reviews of animated films

A   **Aero**

You'll want to see this film again and again, with a wonderful cast of animals, and folk music soundtrack sung by studio performers. And you'll learn something new about the characters each time you watch. Based on the book by a well-known author, it's a favourite for all the family.

B   **Magic Makers**

This is a gentle film about a village of animals who all help each other through life – but things don't always go at all as they expected. In fact, they're usually far better! A beautiful, funny film with great songs you won't forget. You'll never get tired of watching it!

C   Imagining

While you're watching this beautiful film, you'll also be entertained by the wonderful piano and violin music that accompanies it. It's a film for the whole family, including young children, to sit down and see together. And everyone will find that they have something in common with the people in the film.

D   **The Dance**

Although they haven't been together for long, a group of brave dancers decide to put on a performance, and their experiences are both funny and sad. The film's message is particularly suitable for teenagers, and the animation, in the form of old-fashioned cartoons rather than created by computers, is spectacular.

E   **Roundabout**

The pictures are so fantastic, they almost need nothing more than the piano music that accompanies them. The film focuses on some brave friends who come together to support each other in various ways, and the well-known performers saying their words bring something really special to it. The film has lots to teach teenagers.

F   **Terry**

The pop music in this film is great, as it features the voices of top performers. The film follows a friendly tiger in the jungle, who becomes a hero to his friends. This film first came out in the 70s, and the graphics in this beautiful film have changed very little.

G   Rainbow

The whole family will sing along to the songs by well-known performers in this film. Choose which of the characters is most like you – and who's your hero! From the book by teenagers' author Dylan Peters, it's been a favourite with audiences since it came out years ago.

H   **Constanz**

This beautiful film, with simple graphics, is based on the well-known novel, which has become very popular in school classrooms. Although it's full of comedy situations and surprises from beginning to end, the film also has a serious message, and will leave you with something to think about after you've watched it.

Questions 11–15

For each question, choose the correct answer.

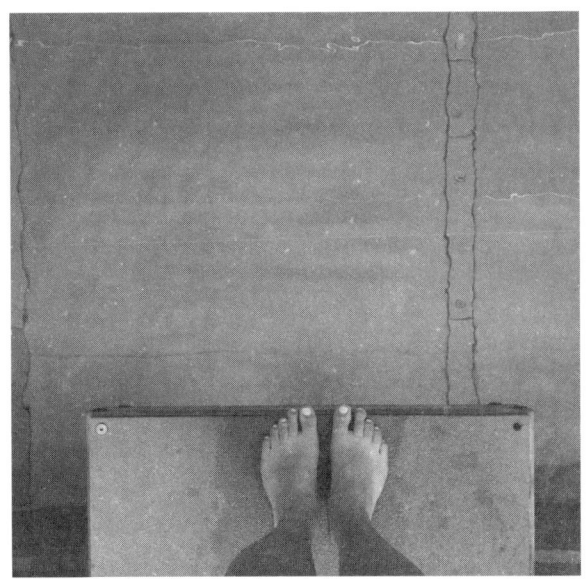

Karina Moore – teenage high diver!

Several times a week, teenager Karina Moore trains at her local pool to jump from the high-diving board into the water – in an attempt to become a national diving champion.

Karina first learned about diving during a family break in Spain, where the resort's pool had a high-diving board. Young people were diving off it, and it looked fun, but Karina didn't join in, even though she was a strong swimmer. Then after returning home, she discovered a long-distance runner she'd always admired had started diving for relaxation – so she became more interested.

Karina joined a beginners' diving class at her local pool. They had several sessions jumping onto soft materials before trying the high board. 'The water looked a long way down,' says Karina, 'but after our training, I felt I'd handle it – without injuring myself! They'd warned me I'd land in the water fast – at around 60 kph – but I was prepared. I couldn't wait to get started – although the others weren't so keen! Anyway, I wasn't disappointed by the experience.'

In Karina's area, there's now lots of interest in high diving, but it's sometimes difficult for swimmers to find suitable practice facilities. Although the pools are deep enough, they're in use so often by diving clubs that other people don't get opportunities to practise. Fortunately, though, Karina's coach noticed her talent and helped her develop her techniques. After only two years, she's winning competitions in her area.

But what's it like to concentrate so much on diving? 'I train 20 hours a week' says Karina, 'and I won't pretend it's easy – you have to enjoy it to spend so much time doing it! It's not easy for my parents either, though – they drive me to training sessions early in the morning, and that costs money. But they've had financial help from sports organisations, luckily. And my schoolwork and social life are good. I still meet my mates – and there's always the phone! The only thing I hadn't realised was that the pool water would damage my hair – I used to love my long hair, but I've had to cut it short because it looked awful! But I'll definitely keep on diving!'

11 What made Karina keen to take up diving?

    A   She wanted to repeat her holiday experience.

    B   She found out her athletics hero had taken it up.

    C   She'd visited a pool where some teenagers were doing it.

    D   She wanted a new challenge after her success at swimming.

12 How did Karina feel the first time she used the high board?

    A   worried about how far it was above the pool

    B   pleased to experience it with other beginners

    C   confident that she wouldn't get hurt

    D   shocked to hit the water at such speed

13 What does the writer suggest about diving facilities in Karina's area?

    A   They're not used as much as they could be.

    B   There aren't enough coaches teaching people to use them.

    C   There aren't as many boards as there used to be.

    D   They're not available to the public for long enough each day.

14 How does Karina feel about spending so much time diving?

    A   surprised by one effect it has had on her

    B   sorry she no longer sees her friends so much

    C   anxious about the amount of money it costs

    D   grateful to be able to focus on something she loves

15 What would the writer say about Karina?

A

She's a young girl who's achieved a lot by becoming a national diving champion – and all with very little support.

B

She's made enormous progress in a very short time – after only a couple of years, she's already showing great signs of success.

C

She has a lot of natural talent, but she's already thinking of having a break from the high board for a while.

D

She's sad that she's given up almost everything for her sport – and her lifestyle really sounds quite hard.

Questions 16–20

Five sentences have been removed from the text below.
For each question, choose the correct answer.
There are three extra sentences which you do not need to use.

Computer game exhibition

Have you ever tried playing the kind of video games that your parents played? The Museum of Science in Manchester, in the UK, has held an exhibition for the last few years, which invites visitors to do exactly that. It offers them the chance to play games from the last 40 years, in various sessions throughout the day.

These video games sessions have now become one of the main attractions of the museum. They are full of people every day, playing a wide range of games.

16 [____] For parents, for example, these are usually the games they used to play in their childhood.

There's also an educational purpose to the games. For instance, some old types of computer, dating back 40 years, are also available in the sessions. They were originally used in classrooms to teach pupils to write their own computer programs.

17 [____] Now, the museum is holding workshops that encourage children to learn similar skills – and they're still very popular.

The sessions are also seen as social events, as people discover how much fun it is to play video games with other family members. And there's also an area at Power Up! where a number of visitors can sit down together. **18** [____] And nowadays, this is often how fans of video games are more likely to experience playing.

The exhibition also shows how much progress technology has made over the last 40 years. Parents can often remember playing very simple games. But the games that are played today are more complex. **19** [____] And the players also have to use much more complicated techniques.

However, one serious side of the exhibition is that organisers also want to show that video gaming is an important industry, employing many skilled people.

20 [____] That way, people who enjoy gaming will also understand all the hard work, talent and imagination that goes into creating these amazing games.

A   Visitors each pay for 90-minute sessions.

B   And at the time, it helped lots of young people to do that.

C   So they hope the exhibition will share this message.

D   But not everyone thinks it's a lot of fun.

E   However, visitors often choose the ones they're familiar with.

F   They have better storylines and animation, too.

G   They also create the music to go with the game.

H   Then they can all enjoy playing the same game.

Questions 21–26

For each question, choose the correct answer.

Music can change the taste of vegetables!

Many children, and some adults too, dislike the taste of certain vegetables. The flavours of foods such as cabbage and broccoli are generally the ones people mention as their least **(21)** .... vegetables, as these vegetables are believed to have an extremely **(22)** .... taste.

However, according to an Oxford psychologist, children might change their **(23)** .... about these foods if they can hear simple music while they're eating – such as the sounds that come from one musical instrument, called a *wind chime*. This instrument often **(24)** .... in people's gardens, and plays sweet notes when the wind blows through it. These notes may make the food seem to taste sweeter than it would do normally.

However, many adults **(25)** .... that their tastes developed as they grew up, so they now enjoy a far greater range of food. As a result, they're much more **(26)** .... to eat the kind of vegetables they always hated during their childhood.

---

21 A pleasant   **B** delicious   **C** special   **D** favourite

22 A bitter   **B** hard   **C** heavy   **D** raw

23 A senses   **B** minds   **C** moods   **D** reasons

24 A drops   **B** connects   **C** attaches   **D** hangs

25 A complain   **B** advise   **C** admit   **D** warn

26 A likely   **B** possible   **C** reasonable   **D** sure

Questions 27–32

For each question, write the correct word.
Write **one** word for each gap.

Hi Marta

How are you? Sorry I haven't written for a while. But now
I have some news – I've got a Saturday job! As you know, I've
(27) .... meaning to look for a job for ages. But then
Mum offered to let (28) .... work in her clothes shop,
so I started last week. I'm really enjoying it, although it's hard
work. There's (29) .... time at all to chat with the other
assistants, sadly. That's (30) .... we're always so busy.

The good thing is that I'm finally earning a bit of money of my own, (31) .... I can use to buy the things I
want. I'm also getting some great work experience.

Why don't you come to the shop (32) .... day soon? It's called Modes, and it's on Green Street. I'm sure
you'll find lots of clothes that you like!

Hope to see you soon.

Janine

You **must** answer this question.
Write your answer in about **100 words** on your answer sheet.

Question 1

Read this email from your English friend Teri and the notes you have made.

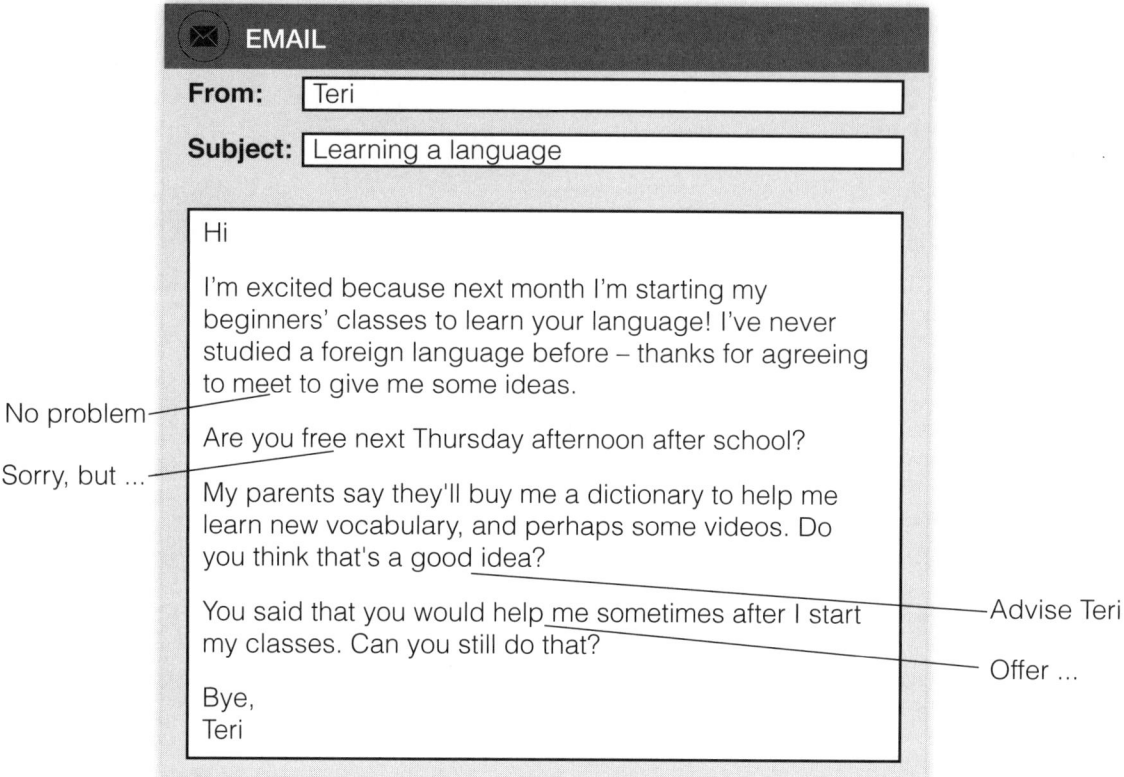

EMAIL

From: Teri

Subject: Learning a language

Hi

I'm excited because next month I'm starting my beginners' classes to learn your language! I've never studied a foreign language before – thanks for agreeing to meet to give me some ideas.

No problem

Are you free next Thursday afternoon after school?

Sorry, but ...

My parents say they'll buy me a dictionary to help me learn new vocabulary, and perhaps some videos. Do you think that's a good idea?

Advise Teri

You said that you would help me sometimes after I start my classes. Can you still do that?

Offer ...

Bye,
Teri

Write your **email** to Teri using **all the notes**.

Choose **one** of these questions.
Write your answer in about **100 words** on the answer sheet.

Question 2

You see this notice in your school English-language magazine.

> **Articles wanted!**
>
> **BEING HEALTHY**
>
> Write an article about young people and healthy living. Is it important for young people to do sport and to keep fit? Why?
>
> What are some fun ways to stay healthy?
>
> The best articles answering these questions will be published next month.

Write your **article**.

Question 3

Your English teacher has asked you to write a story. Your story must begin with this sentence:

It was my turn to go on stage to perform in the talent competition.

Write your **story**.

Questions 1–7

For each question, choose the correct answer.

1 Which was the girl's favourite film?

A

B

C

2 What did the boy see at the transport museum?

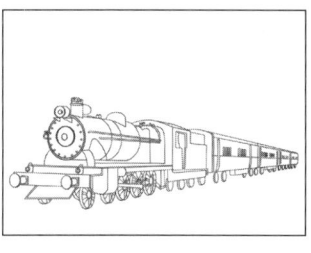

A

B

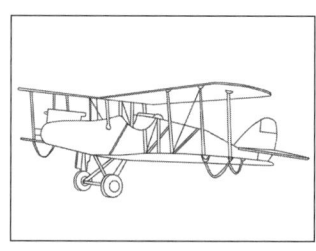

C

3 Where does the girl hope her family will go on holiday?

A

B

C

4 What did the girl lose at the show?

A

B

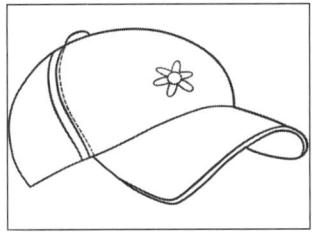

C

5 Which appointment did the boy have today?

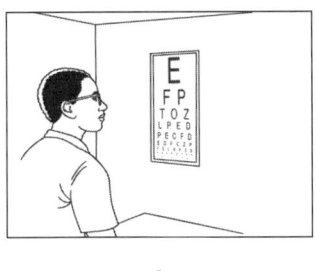

A

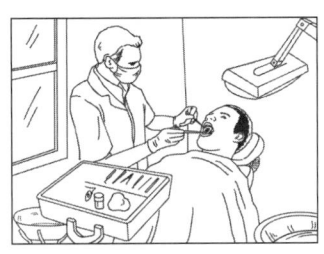

B

C

6 Which book can the girl collect today?

A

B

C

7 Which sport is the boy going to try?

A

B

C

🎧 **Questions 8–13**

43 For each question, choose the correct answer.

....

8   You will hear two friends talking about a play.
    Why did the girl leave the theatre early?

    A   She felt unwell.

    B   She hated the play.

    C   She had an appointment.

9   You will hear two friends talking about the food at a school party.
    They agree that

    A   there was lots of variety.

    B   everything there was tasty.

    C   the food they took was popular.

10 You will hear two friends talking about a soccer match they both watched on TV.
    Why was the boy disappointed?

    A   The team he supports lost.

    B   His favourite player was injured.

    C   The quality of the match was bad.

11 You will hear two friends talking about a new science building at their school.
    They agree that

    A   it looks great from the outside.

    B   the equipment is very good.

    C   it is very well decorated.

12 You will hear a girl talking about a blog she has started writing.
    How does she feel about it?

    A   delighted that other people like it

    B   surprised it was so easy to set up

    C   satisfied with its appearance

13 You will hear a girl telling her friend about learning Chinese.
    The boy suggests that the girl should

    A   use websites to help her.

    B   find a conversation class.

    C   buy a good textbook.

🎧 **Questions 14–19**

44 For each question, write the correct answer in the gap.
Write **one** or **two words** or a **number** or a **date** or a **time**.

You will hear a student giving some information to his class about an acting club he's a member of.

My acting club

Teacher:

Appeared on TV as a **(14)** ....

Has mostly appeared in **(15)** .... shows

Sessions:

First part – using your **(16)** .... well

Second part – practising performance skills

Take place at the **(17)** ....

Acting Club play:

Called **(18)** '..'

First performance – on **(19)** ....

Questions 20–25

45 For each question, choose the correct answer.

You will hear an interview with a girl called Jasmine, talking about her experiences of flying a plane.

20 Why did Jasmine decide to try a flying experience day?

    A   Someone recommended it.

    B   She wants to become a pilot.

    C   To see her area from high up.

21 How did Jasmine feel at the beginning of the flying experience day?

    A   nervous about making mistakes

    B   worried about how small the plane was

    C   disappointed with the arrangements

22 What did Jasmine think about the training she did before the flight?

    A   It was badly presented.

    B   It was done too quickly.

    C   Some of it wasn't useful.

23 Jasmine says that during the flight her instructor

    A   said very little.

    B   stayed very calm.

    C   joked with her a lot.

24 Jasmine says that the flight

    A   made her feel tired.

    B   seemed to last a long time.

    C   was better than she had hoped.

25 Which experience day would Jasmine like to try most?

    A   horse riding

    B   deep-sea fishing

    C   sports car driving

PART 1

(2–3 minutes)

Phase 1

Good morning / afternoon / evening

What's your name?

How old are you?

Where do you live?

Who do you live with?

Phase 2

(possible examiner questions)

Tell us about your favourite food and drink.

What did you do yesterday?

Do you like playing computer games? (Why? / Why not?)

Which famous person would you like to meet? (Why?)

Which shops do you like going to? (Why?)

What's the best holiday you've ever had? (Why was it so good?)

Tell us about your English classes.

Which sport would you like to try in the future? (Why?)

PART 2

(3–5 minutes)

Now I'd like each of you to talk on your own about something. I'm going to give each of you a photograph and I'd like you to talk about it.

A, here is your photograph. It shows some people **doing an activity on a sunny day**. (See page C3.)

B, you just listen.

A, please tell us what you can see in the photograph.

B, here is your photograph. It shows someone **getting ready for school**. (See page C4.)

A, you just listen.

B, please tell us what you can see in the photograph.

PART 3

(4–5 minutes)

Now, in this part of the test you're going to talk about something together for about two minutes. I'm going to describe a situation to you.

A girl's penfriend is visiting her from another country. The girl would like to buy her penfriend **a present** that will remind her of her stay.

Here are some presents she could buy. (See page C13.)

Talk together about the different **presents** she could buy her penfriend and say **which would be best**.

All right? Now, talk together.

PART 4

(3–4 minutes)

Which of these presents would you prefer to have? (Why?)

Do you like giving presents to people? (Why? / Why not?)

What was the last present you bought for someone?

What's the best present you've ever received? (Why?)

When do people give presents in your country? (Why?)

Questions 1–5

For each question, choose the correct answer.

1

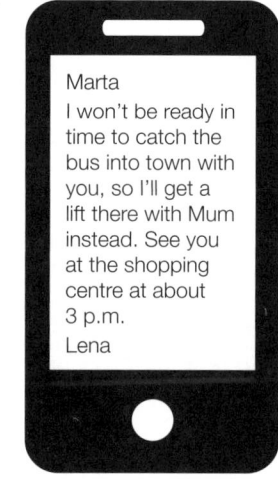

Marta
I won't be ready in time to catch the bus into town with you, so I'll get a lift there with Mum instead. See you at the shopping centre at about 3 p.m.
Lena

Lena is

A   suggesting that Marta travels into town without her.

B   offering Marta a lift into town instead of catching the bus.

C   checking the time she arranged to meet Marta at the shopping centre.

2

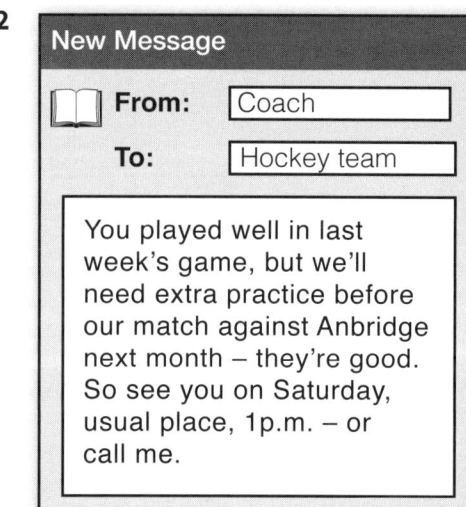

New Message

From: Coach

To: Hockey team

You played well in last week's game, but we'll need extra practice before our match against Anbridge next month – they're good. So see you on Saturday, usual place, 1p.m. – or call me.

A   The coach needs team members to tell him if they're available for a match.

B   The coach wants to help the team improve their performance before they play again.

C   The coach is congratulating the netball team for winning their game last week.

3

Please give staff at the desk your college student number before using any of the computers in the Study Centre.

A Staff at the desk will show you how to use the computers here.

B These computers are reserved only for students at this college.

C If you're not a college student, ask staff for permission to use a computer.

4

Tom
The sports shop called – the one on Hatton Street. They've finally repaired your tennis racket! Will you have time to collect it, or shall I do it on my way home from work?
Mum

What does Mum want to know?

A how to find the sports shop that's repaired Tom's racket

B whether the sports shop will still be open when she finishes work

C if Tom is going to be available to pick up his racket

5

Milton Music Store
Second-hand guitars and violins for sale.
Very reasonable prices.
New instruments also available.
Call: 08413 672 521

A This store has more second-hand instruments available than new ones.

B You can only buy instruments here that other people have already used.

C This store doesn't charge a lot for instruments that aren't new.

Questions 6–10

For each question, choose the correct answer.

The people below are all doing school geography projects and want to find a website to help them.
On the opposite page there are descriptions of eight geography websites.
Decide which website would be the most suitable for the people below.

6 Sandra wants to learn more about what Planet Earth is actually made of, and how much of it is covered by water. She'd also like online advice about how to organise her work.

7 Miranda wants to learn about some of the famous tourist sites in the world, and why they have become famous. She'd like to play games on the website to help her remember the information.

8 For his project, Billy needs to find out about the biggest mountains in the world, and the kind of animals living near them. He'd also like to see videos of the locations he's studying.

9 Anna wants to learn about the biggest land areas of the world, and get key facts about their geography. She'd also like advice on how to improve her map-reading skills.

10 Kristofer's country has very cold winters, so he's interested in how other people in cold countries deal with their environment. He'd like to share his experiences online with teenagers there.

Geography websites

A   **Geoview**

This website has fantastic videos of animals in challenging locations, and information about how they manage to live there. There are also helpful tips on understanding geographical information, such as maps and diagrams of the Earth and its oceans. Users can also share information about useful links to follow.

B   **Geographical**

This website has lots of maps, quizzes and advice, to check your knowledge of what you've studied – and remind you of anything you've forgotten! There's a brilliant section about popular places in many different countries, which attract large numbers of visitors, with background historical details about the reasons these places are now so well known.

C   Geography.com

This website has interesting maps and details about places that have become famous tourist destinations in different countries, and also some famous geographical features around the world, such as the biggest mountains and rivers. There are also online tips available on how to research information for projects.

D   **Goworld**

How do people live in places with very high or low temperatures in different seasons? Find out how people adapt to the climate they live in, how it affects their lives and what they do to stay warm or keep cool, as necessary. You can also upload your own stories about life in extreme temperatures in your country.

E   **Planet Zoom**

Not sure how to understand the information included on maps? Here's a step-by-step guide to using them! The site also has games and puzzles about all the continents, including Africa, Asia and Europe, and important details about them, such as their huge size, and their mountain ranges, rivers and climate.

F   **Worldwide**

This website has lots of beautiful photos, maps and film clips to help you learn more about some of the highest – and coldest – peaks on the planet. You'll find plenty of amazing facts about them, together with details of the wildlife that makes its home in the surrounding areas.

G   GeoInfo

Which countries in the world have the coldest winters, the highest mountains or the most unusual animals? Check your knowledge with some fantastic geography puzzles and games. And the photos on this site also show people's everyday lives in very different climate conditions.

H   **Geowatch**

What's underneath the ground we walk on? You'll find maps and diagrams here to tell you – including what you'd see inside the planet if you cut it in half! There's information, too, about parts of the world that aren't land, but actually oceans and seas, and help on researching and presenting project information.

Questions 11–15

For each question, choose the correct answer.

Cross-country skiing in Sweden

by Jenna Walton, aged 15

Last year, Mum and I wanted to try a winter sport called cross-country skiing – travelling on skis across the countryside. And pictures of one area in Sweden, with people skiing along through forests on wonderful white snow, persuaded us that destination was a good choice. We hadn't done much skiing, though, so weren't sure how difficult cross-country skiing was, compared with skiing fast down steep mountains. But we signed up to join a group of people, of all ages, plus a guide.

We'd read about the place we went to before we left, so we knew it was close to where Sweden ends and Norway starts. And our family knew we couldn't text home, as there was no internet connection – and actually, it was relaxing to be far from anywhere, or anyone. What we hadn't realised was that from there, we'd be able to see amazing coloured lights in the sky, which appeared at certain times of year, called the Northern Lights – what a sight!

On our first day there, I hated getting up in the dark, but it meant I saw the sun come up over the forest, so I was glad I did. And sunshine was forecast for the week, I was delighted to hear! But the real problem was my 15kg rucksack, full of food and clothes – I had no idea it would weigh that much. Anyway, we skied for hours across mainly flat snow. Having special light skis was supposed to help us climb the few hills there were – although I still couldn't do it!

Finally we stopped for the night. It wasn't until we'd reached our hut that our guide mentioned we'd just crossed a frozen lake to get there – but nothing surprised us by that point! Anyway, he gave us all jobs to do – cutting fire wood and cooking food – and soon we were having dinner, made from whatever food we'd brought – a strange mix, but it tasted delicious. And everywhere was so peaceful outside that none of us stayed awake long.

Mum and I want to try another winter sports trip, maybe snowboarding. But we'll probably end up just as exhausted as we were after this trip!

11 Jenna and her mum decided to go cross-country skiing in Sweden because

    A   they wanted a change from mountain skiing holidays.

    B   they'd heard the sport would be easier than skiing down hills.

    C   they'd met a group of people who wanted to go, too.

    D   they found a place there that they were keen to visit.

12 After their arrival, what did they discover about where they were staying?

    A   It wasn't far from the border with another country.

    B   They could get great views of a spectacular natural event.

    C   It was at a point where they couldn't use technology.

    D   They weren't near local people or their homes.

13 How did Jenna feel about the long trips through the snow on skis?

    A   surprised she had to carry such a heavy bag

    B   pleased about the weight of the skis she was given

    C   glad that going uphill wasn't as hard as she'd thought

    D   worried the good weather they were having wouldn't last

14 Regarding their accommodation, Jenna says everyone

    A   had difficulties getting to sleep there.

    B   was unhappy at the quality of the food.

    C   had to help out with all the housework.

    D   was shocked to hear details of their journey there.

15 What would Jenna text to a friend about her trip?

A

> One reason we chose this trip was that we thought we'd be among loads of trees, which we love – but that hasn't happened so far.

B

> The people in our group were really friendly – but they were all Mum's age and older, really.

C

> I'm not used to getting out of bed so early to do things! But it was worth it, as the sunrise was wonderful.

D

> Mum and I have agreed that although the trip was great, we might attempt something less tiring on our next winter holiday.

Questions 16–20

Five sentences have been removed from the text below. For each question, choose the correct answer.
There are three extra sentences which you do not need to use.

The giant piano

A young man in New Zealand recently became famous for making one of the largest pianos ever.

Adrian Mann, who now works as a professional piano builder, started building the piano when he was just 16 years old, and made many of the parts for it himself. The piano is 5.7 metres long and is very heavy. And the keyboard actually has keys that are a metre in length. **16** But despite this difference in size, the instrument can still be played perfectly, thanks to Adrian's hard work.

17 In fact, the whole thing started when Adrian became interested in the materials used for the wires inside the piano. These create the notes when they're hit.

And he found that if the wires were really long, he could get an amazing sound. From there, he went on to build the whole piano.

The instrument was kept inside a church in his town for some time, before Adrian decided it was time to transfer the huge piano from the church to his workshop. **18** So in the end, the fire service had to come and help take the instrument to its new home.

Since the move, a lot of piano players have visited Adrian to try out the piano. But Adrian says that when they arrive, some people aren't very positive about the piano.

19 But actually, it always performs brilliantly. They soon discover that the piano can play a wide range of music, just like any normal piano.

There's been so much interest in Adrian's piano that he could probably start making and selling others just like it. **20** So, at the moment, he has no plans to make any more.

A However, he put a lot of work into his original model.

B It's so big, you could imagine actually lying down inside it!

C So what gave Adrian the idea to create such a huge piano?

D They expect that the instrument won't sound very good.

E But things weren't always that simple.

F That's much larger than on a normal-sized piano.

G Most of them were surprised by the wonderful result.

H But he soon found he couldn't move it out on his own.

Questions 21–26

For each question, choose the correct answer.

Clever birds

The wild birds known as ravens are thought to be very clever. In fact, they can solve some quite **(21)** .... problems, especially when they're trying to get food. For example, one bird was filmed taking a box of nuts from a bird table and **(22)** .... it onto the ground, so that it would break and the bird could eat the nuts inside!

Scientists also **(23)** .... that the birds could actually use stones as tools to **(24)** .... out simple tasks. So in an experiment, they taught five birds to use a tool to open a box with food inside. The birds soon became very **(25)** .... at doing this. So for the next experiment, the birds were given a small **(26)** .... of tools to choose from. They always picked the tool that scientists had given them for the first task. And hours later, they could still remember which tool they'd used!

21   A   expert   B   complicated   C   heavy   D   confused

22   A   letting   B   falling   C   dropping   D   leaving

23   A   noticed   B   advised   C   watched   D   studied

24   A   take   B   carry   C   make   D   check

25   A   experienced   B   intelligent   C   correct   D   keen

26   A   group   B   total   C   amount   D   number

Questions 27–32

For each question, write the correct word.
Write **one** word for each gap.

My thoughts on how to write
by Sarah Beecham

Welcome to my blog! That's for anyone who's new and
has **(27)** .... visited this site before! But if you
(28) .... seen some of my blogs, then you'll know
like sharing ideas about creative writing and how to do it.

At the moment, I'm sitting at my desk in my room,
(29) .... I do most of my writing. I love writing stories, but not every day. I'll often update my diary or
something, too – and this blog, **(30)** .... course ! But I have a notebook of things I would like to include in
my writing and new words I like the sound of.

But I recently discovered the most important thing is just to **(31)** .... going once you've started writing.
And **(32)** .... doesn't matter how bad your writing is at the beginning, because you can always go back
and make improvements. In fact, that's the part I enjoy most!

You **must** answer this question.
Write your answer in about **100 words** on the answer sheet.

....

Question 1

Read this email from your English-speaking friend Corey and the notes you have made.

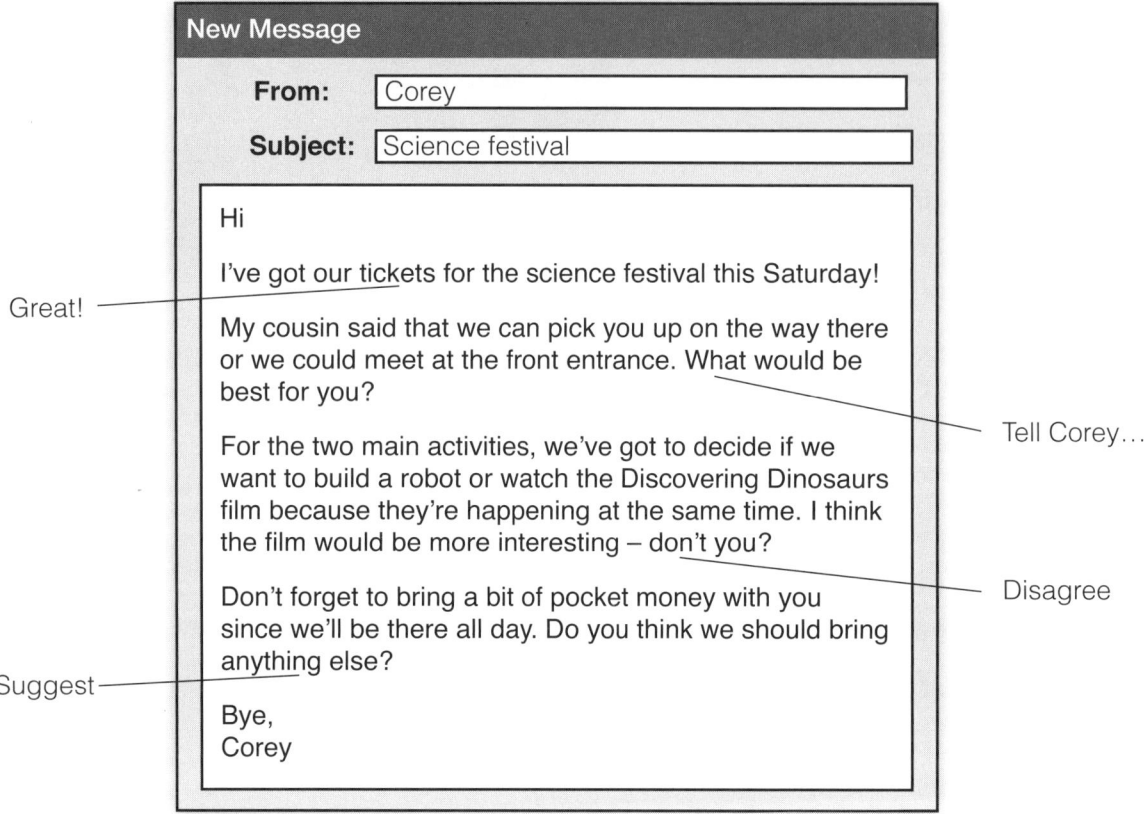

Write your **email** to Corey using **all the notes**.

Choose **one** of these questions.
Write your answer in about **100 words** on the answer sheet.

....

Question 2

You see this notice on an international English website for young people.

Articles wanted!

FESTIVALS
Write an article telling us about
a festival that you or your family
celebrate. When does the festival
take place, and what happens?
What do you like about it?
The best articles answering these
questions will be published
next month.

Write your **article**.

Question 3

Your English teacher has asked you to write a story. Your story must begin with this sentence:

As my friend and I arrived at school yesterday morning, we saw something incredible!

Write your **story**.

Questions 1–7

46 For each question, choose the correct answer.

---

1 Which coat did the girl buy?

A

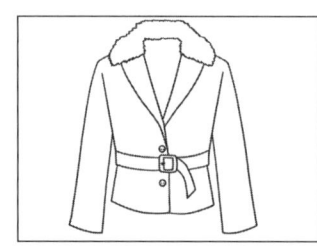

B

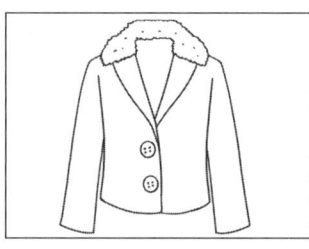

C

2 Which musical instrument would the boy prefer to learn?

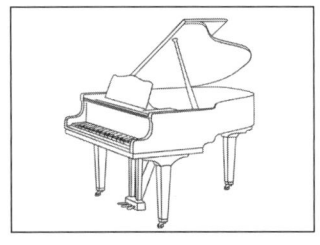

A

B

C

3 What does the girl miss about her old apartment?

A

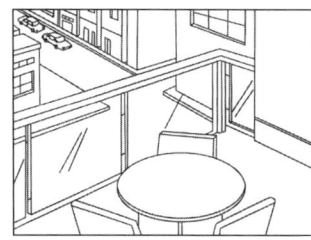

B

C

4   Which sport does the boy not do any more?

A

B

C

5   Who has won the school poetry competition?

A

B

C

6   Which programme is on TV next?

A

B

C

7   What present is the girl going to buy for her mum's birthday?

A

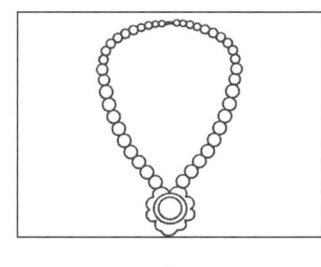

B

C

Questions 8–13

47   For each question, choose the correct answer.

8   You will hear two friends talking about travelling into the town centre.
Why does the girl prefer taking the bus to the town centre?

   A   There's a bus stop hear her home.

   B   She meets someone she knows on it.

   C   The service is very frequent.

9   You will hear two friends talking about a music video they've seen.
The friends agree that

   A   the song is excellent.

   B   the dancing is original.

   C   the video is well made.

10   You will hear two friends talking about buying a mobile phone.
The boy thinks the girl should

   A   get the newest model.

   B   go to the phone shop.

   C   look at lots of reviews.

11   You will hear two friends talking about school.
The girl is feeling pleased because she

   A   was given a reward for her school work.

   B   was chosen to play in a sports match.

   C   got a high mark for her homework.

12   You will hear a boy telling his friend about a family visit to some relatives.
How did he feel about it?

   A   worried that he annoyed someone

   B   upset that they stayed so long

   C   sorry when they had to leave

13   You will hear two friends talking about a new swimming pool.
What did the girl like best about it?

   A   The water is very warm.

   B   There are fun things to do.

   C   Lots of young people use it.

Questions 14–19

48   For each question, write the correct answer in the gap.
Write **one** or **two words** or a **number** or a **date** or a **time**.

You will hear a student called Matilde giving a presentation to her class about a science museum she visited.

Science museum visit

Matilde's favourite room contained displays about **(14)** ....

The **(15)** .... exhibition is currently closed.

Matilde made a **(16)** .... at the museum.

The shop had a really good range of **(17)** ....

The guided tour lasts for **(18)** .... minutes.

Visitors must use the entrance on **(19)** .... Road.

Questions 20–25

49   For each question, choose the correct answer.

....

You will hear an interview with a 17-year-old boy called Erik who went cycling across the USA with his dad.

20   Erik and his dad wanted to do a long cycle ride to
   A   make money for charity.
   B   break their usual routine.
   C   spend lots of time together.

21   Why did they choose to cycle in the USA and not in other countries?
   A   To avoid difficulties with language.
   B   They thought it would be safer.
   C   It was easier to organise.

22   How did Erik feel as they were setting off?
   A   surprised at how relaxed they were
   B   excited about all the things they'd see
   C   nervous they wouldn't succeed

23   Erik's favourite days were those on which
   A   they didn't cycle as far as usual.
   B   the weather was warm and dry.
   C   they had a chance to be sociable.

24   Erik says that during the ride, he and his dad
   A   talked about many personal issues.
   B   became comfortable with silence.
   C   disagreed about many things.

25   In the future, Erik plans to
   A   start taking part in races.
   B   go on another long ride.
   C   only cycle during his free time.

PART 1

(2–3 minutes)

Phase 1

Good morning / afternoon / evening

What's your name?

How old are you?

Where do you live?

Who do you live with?

Phase 2

(possible examiner questions)

How do you usually keep in touch with your friends? (Why?)

Tell us about your favourite teacher.

What kinds of things do you like reading? (Why?)

What are you going to do this evening? (Why?)

Do you prefer to eat at home or in a restaurant? (Why?)

Do you help your parents with jobs around the house? (Why? / Why not?)

What would you like to study in the future? (Why?)

How often do you go to the cinema? (Why?)

PART 2

(3–5 minutes)

Now I'd like each of you to talk on your own about something. I'm going to give each of you a photograph and I'd like you to talk about it.

A, here is your photograph. It shows **a family doing a holiday activity together**. (See page C3.)

B, you just listen.

A, please tell us what you can see in the photograph.

B, here is your photograph. It shows **a family preparing a meal together**. (See page C4.)

A, you just listen.

B, please tell us what you can see in the photograph.

PART 3

(4–5 minutes)

Now, in this part of the test you're going to talk about something together for about two minutes. I'm going to describe a situation to you.

A teacher has asked her class for ideas of **places** to go on a class trip. The place must be fun, but also be somewhere that students can learn something.

Here are some places they could go to. (See page C14.)

Talk together about the different **places** they could go to and say **which would be best**.

All right? Now, talk together.

PART 4

(3–4 minutes)

What kinds of places do you like visiting? (Why?)

Do you visit places with your school? (Tell us about the last place you visited with your school. / Where would you like to visit?)

What's the most interesting place to visit in your city? (Why?)

Where in the world would you most like to visit? (Why?)

Is it important for schools to take students on school trips? (Why? / Why not?)

Questions 1–5

For each question, choose the correct answer.

1

New Message

From: Mrs Evans

To: All students

Could everyone involved in the school performance for parents tomorrow please meet in the hall at 4 p.m. today for the final practice?

A Mrs Evans wants to check who is taking part in the performance this afternoon.

B Mrs Evans wants everyone to practise their performance again before the audience sees it.

C Mrs Evans is letting students know that parents are coming to the practice tomorrow.

2

PLEASE DON'T FEED BREAD TO THE DUCKS!

AVAILABLE FOR SALE INSIDE LAKE SHOP:

SPECIAL FOOD PERMITTED FOR BIRDS

A If you need bread during your visit, it's available for sale inside the shop.

B Feeding the birds on the lake is not allowed unless you have special permission.

C Visitors are encouraged not to give the birds anything apart from proper bird food.

3

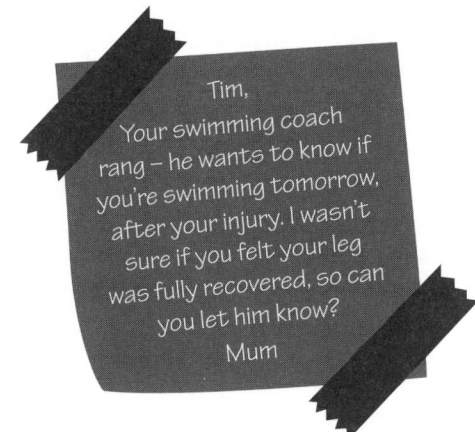

Tim,
Your swimming coach rang – he wants to know if you're swimming tomorrow, after your injury. I wasn't sure if you felt your leg was fully recovered, so can you let him know?
Mum

A   Tim must decide whether he's well enough to swim after his injury.

B   Tim's mum doesn't think Tim is fit and ready to go swimming yet.

C   Tim needs to inform his swimming coach that he's injured his leg.

4

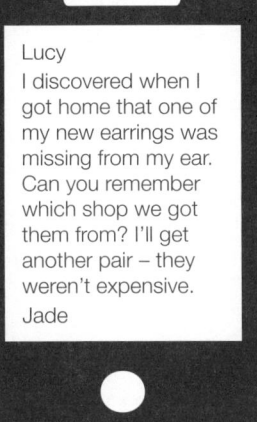

Lucy
I discovered when I got home that one of my new earrings was missing from my ear. Can you remember which shop we got them from? I'll get another pair – they weren't expensive.
Jade

Jade wants Lucy to

A   tell Jade if she knows where a missing item is.

B   accompany Jade on a shopping trip into town.

C   help Jade to replace something she's lost.

5

Art Room closed –
heating problems.
See Mr James in Room B16
to check where your
art lessons will be.

A   Art classes will be in Room B16 as the Art Room is too cold.

B   To find out which room to go to for art lessons, ask Mr James.

C   Mr James is taking all art lessons until problems in the Art Room are fixed.

Questions 6–10

For each question, choose the correct answer.

The people below all want to find a beach to go to at the weekend.
On the opposite page there are descriptions of eight beaches.
Decide which beach would be the most suitable for the people below.

6   Neil and his family want a beach that's close to a car park and offers several other activities apart from spending time in the sea. They'd also like a picnic area near the beach.

7   Jack and Henry can swim well, so they'd like opportunities for distance swimming with their dad. Their mum wants to go riding on the beach, and also buy snacks for everyone there.

8   Salma and Katia want to go somewhere they can try watersports for the first time. Their mum wants a beach with warm water, and organised activities suitable for their small sister.

9   Anna and her family would like to do some sunbathing, but also have a long walk along the coast. Anna also wants to try doing some sand sculptures.

10   Sylvie's family want a beach suitable for Sylvie's small sister to go swimming, as she's only just learned. Sylvie wants somewhere with various organised games and activities, where she can meet other people her age.

Beaches

A   Holly Bay

The café here serves delicious meals and sandwiches! The water's calm in the bay, perfect for people wanting to swim across it – around 2 kms! However, it's very deep, so is only suitable for strong swimmers. There are often sand artists here, and horses for hire to take you along the beach.

B   Franscombe

This beach is popular with families with young children and people who aren't strong swimmers, as the water is warm and not deep. Bring your own food to the picnic area, or try the great snacks at the café. However, the nearest car park is quite a walk away.

C   Barmouth Beach

This beach often has displays of animals and birds – skilfully made from sand, which you can also learn how to do. It's also the perfect place for lying in the sun – or why not explore the beach paths on foot for an hour or two? The views are fantastic.

D   Westley Beach

There are distance swimming, sailing and surfing sessions for people of all levels, and the beach is also famous for sculptures made of sand, which artists display every weekend! It's easily reached from the car park through a lovely wood, which you can explore on foot when it gets cooler.

E   Minton Strand

The sea here offers safe swimming and sailing, even for beginners, but there's still plenty to do when you want a change from sunbathing. A teenagers' beach club offers sports like cycle rides, volleyball and beach chess – great for everyone getting to know each other!

F   South Beach

This beautiful beach offers safe swimming. And when you fancy a change from sunbathing or watersports, there's a funfair nearby, and beautiful gardens to walk through, with tables and chairs where you can eat your own food. Leave your car by the gardens, and you'll be on the beach almost immediately.

G   Silver Sands

This beach has a sea temperature slightly higher than other coastal areas, and with its gentle waves it's perfect for children. There's plenty to do, too, with play leaders offering games to entertain younger ones, and surfing and sailing available at all levels, including beginners. The snack bar is excellent, too.

H   Maple Sands

Adults keen on horses love this beach, with its daily riding sessions. At certain times, the sea leaves warm-water pools on the beach, perfect for children to play in, but the water further out is deeper, for more challenging swimming. And the teenagers' beach club offers group activities, like making sand sculptures – great for making new friends!

Questions 11–15

For each question, choose the correct answer.

Our school newspaper
by Michael Williams

Some years ago, our head teacher, Mrs Waters, decided to start a school newspaper, and get as many students as possible to take on the job of producing it – and parents, too. She felt the newspaper would help them learn more about school life, through articles on things like sports achievements and arts projects, which not all students know about if they're not taking part. Students took the whole thing very seriously – and we now have a prize-winning newspaper!

Some of my friends joined the newspaper team immediately and enjoyed it. I'd always loved creative writing and drawing cartoons, which I thought would be perfect in the newspaper, so I signed up. My dad, who's a journalist, was pleased – he thought that even though I wasn't keen on a job like his, the newspaper would be a great opportunity for me. And he was right – I loved it! Dad often came along to give advice, which was popular with the students. It was difficult sometimes, if he was busy, but he learned a lot about the school that way.

My first job was writing a report about a sports event – a writing style I'd never attempted before. But Dad reminded me it was similar in some ways to writing a story – getting information in the right order. Once I'd understood that, there was no stopping me – and after my first efforts, I developed quite a professional style, which was brilliant. Sometimes the team couldn't use what I'd written, or my cartoons, for whatever reason, but I didn't mind. And sometimes it was hard to finish stuff on time, but I usually got there.

I'm now one of the editors – we decide what goes into the newspaper, so our names no longer appear in print. And it's stressful sometimes as we don't have much time, but we try to manage that properly. We also correct mistakes in people's articles, which we all had to get used to, but we were soon doing it without thinking – and in our own schoolwork, too. I still put off calling people outside school for comments on stuff, but I guess it's all good experience – at least, that's what Dad says!

11 Michael's head teacher wanted to start a student newspaper to

   A   provide an activity for students not interested in sport or art.

   B   make students feel more confident about taking part in something.

   C   keep students better informed about what was happening at school.

   D   give students the experience of being responsible for something.

12 Michael decided to join the newspaper because

   A   he had ideas about some work he could do for it.

   B   he was considering a career in journalism.

   C   his friends had encouraged him to do so.

   D   he liked the idea of being part of a team.

13 When Michael first started working on the newspaper, he was

   A   disappointed when his stories sometimes weren't used.

   B   delighted at the way his writing skills improved.

   C   pleased to find he could make use of his art skills.

   D   worried he'd be late completing some of his writing.

14 What does Michael say about his role on the newspaper now?

   A   He feels uncomfortable about correcting other students' work.

   B   He still needs to improve the way he manages his time.

   C   He's happier to handle making telephone calls to others.

   D   He's become better at making articles more accurate.

15 What would Michael's dad say about the newspaper?

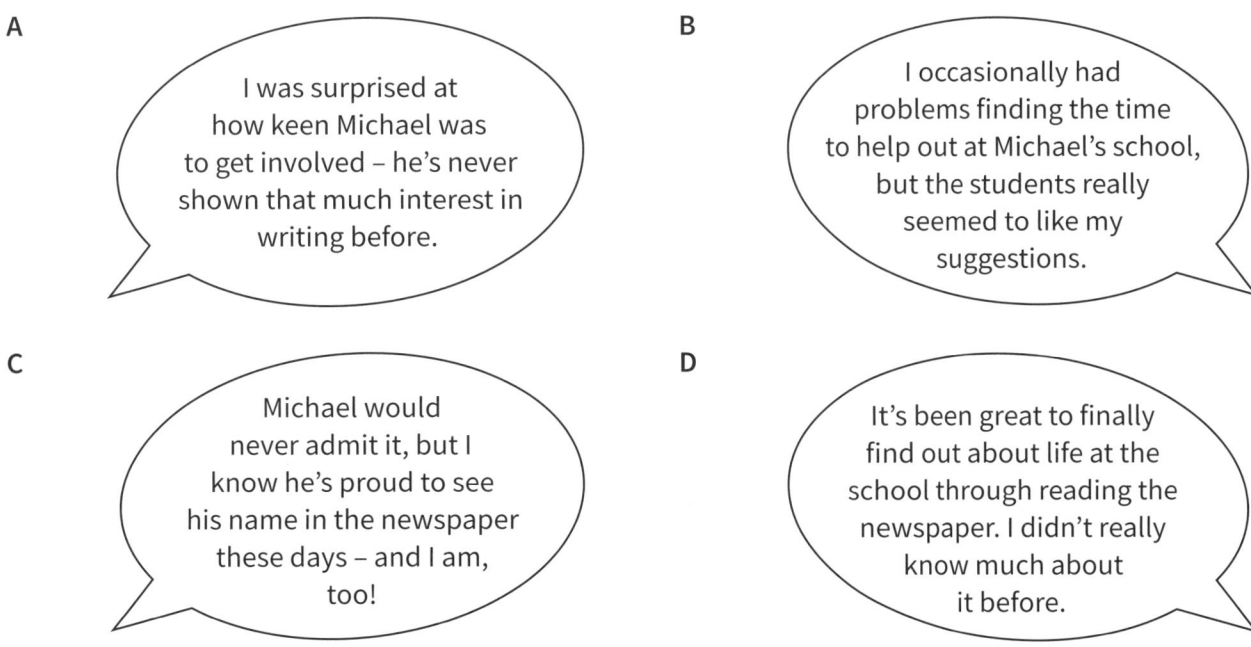

A
I was surprised at how keen Michael was to get involved – he's never shown that much interest in writing before.

B
I occasionally had problems finding the time to help out at Michael's school, but the students really seemed to like my suggestions.

C
Michael would never admit it, but I know he's proud to see his name in the newspaper these days – and I am, too!

D
It's been great to finally find out about life at the school through reading the newspaper. I didn't really know much about it before.

Questions 16–20

Five sentences have been removed from the text below. For each question, choose the correct answer.
There are three extra sentences which you do not need to use.

A new way of making electricity

Ever since the 19th century, when people were developing different ways of creating electricity, companies have looked for improved ways of producing power, using cleaner and more efficient methods.

Now a UK company called Pavegen has been working on technology that could be widely used in the future to produce electricity. **16** ____ The company has developed a special type of floor, made of square tiles. Underneath each square, there's a system that can produce a certain amount of electricity very cheaply – from the energy created every time someone steps on it!

The creator of the floor, Laurence Kemball-Cook, came up with the idea when he was a student, and did some work experience with an energy company. The company asked him to investigate ways of providing street lighting in city centres, using energy from the sun to produce electricity. **17** ____ One reason was that many city centres don't get enough sunlight, because of all the tall buildings. Then he thought of a better plan.

18 ____ The right technology could be used to convert this energy into electricity – right under people's feet!

The design of the floor is actually extremely effective. **19** ____ And the reason is that a lot of energy is produced simply because of the large numbers of people walking across the floor. In fact, the special squares are already in place in several locations with high numbers of pedestrians. These include big department stores and also an airport.

The flooring can have other uses too, such as recording how many people visit a shopping centre at particular times. **20** ____ For example, shop owners in the centre would be interested in knowing at which times of days they have the highest customer numbers. So the next time you visit a big shopping centre, have a careful look at the floor that you're walking across!

A   But that isn't the end of the story.

B   This kind of information is very useful for certain people.

C   Why not use the energy created by pedestrians instead?

D   However, one big problem could be cost.

E   And it's actually based on a simple idea.

F   This is especially true when it's been used in very busy areas.

G   But it soon became clear that this might not work.

H   This new system should work even better.

Questions 21–26

For each question, choose the correct answer.

Colouring books

Many people probably used to spend time adding colour to pictures in colouring books when they were children. However, once people get older, very few of them continue with the hobby. Instead, they **(21)** .... their crayons away in the cupboard forever.

However, psychology researchers now think that even for adults, **(22)** .... as little as ten minutes a day colouring pictures in this way can bring huge **(23)** .... For example, some people say that it improves their **(24)** .... for a while by making them feel more cheerful and generally calmer.

One reason for this may be that other activities **(25)** .... with art, such as drawing or painting, can actually be quite stressful, especially if you don't feel very successful at it. But adding colour to a picture that's already drawn for you **(26)** .... only a low level of skill, so you can relax rather than becoming anxious about it!

21	**A** leave	**B** set	**C** give	**D** put
22	**A** taking	**B** completing	**C** spending	**D** filling
23	**A** benefits	**B** interests	**C** favours	**D** uses
24	**A** character	**B** mood	**C** condition	**D** mind
25	**A** connected	**B** joined	**C** compared	**D** attached
26	**A** depends	**B** calls	**C** lacks	**D** requires

Questions 27–32

For each question, write the correct word.
Write **one** word for each gap.

Hi Karina,

Guess what! I've finally joined the local girls' football team in my town! As you know, it's something I've wanted to do (27) .... ages, so I'm glad I've finally signed up.

I think my parents were a bit surprised, though, as I'd never really taken very (28) .... interest in sport, but after watching a women's football match on TV, I just knew it was for me.

I've attended football training every week (29) .... then, and last Saturday I played in my first match. It was really exciting! And (30) .... of the best things was that I actually scored a goal! We didn't go on to win the match, but our coach was still really pleased with our performance.

Our next match is on 25th. You're not on holiday with your parents then, (31) .... you? So why don't you come along and watch? It would (32) .... great to see you!

Samantha

You must answer this question.

Write your answer in about **100 words** on the answer sheet.

Question 1

Read this email from your English-speaking friend Alex and the notes you have made.

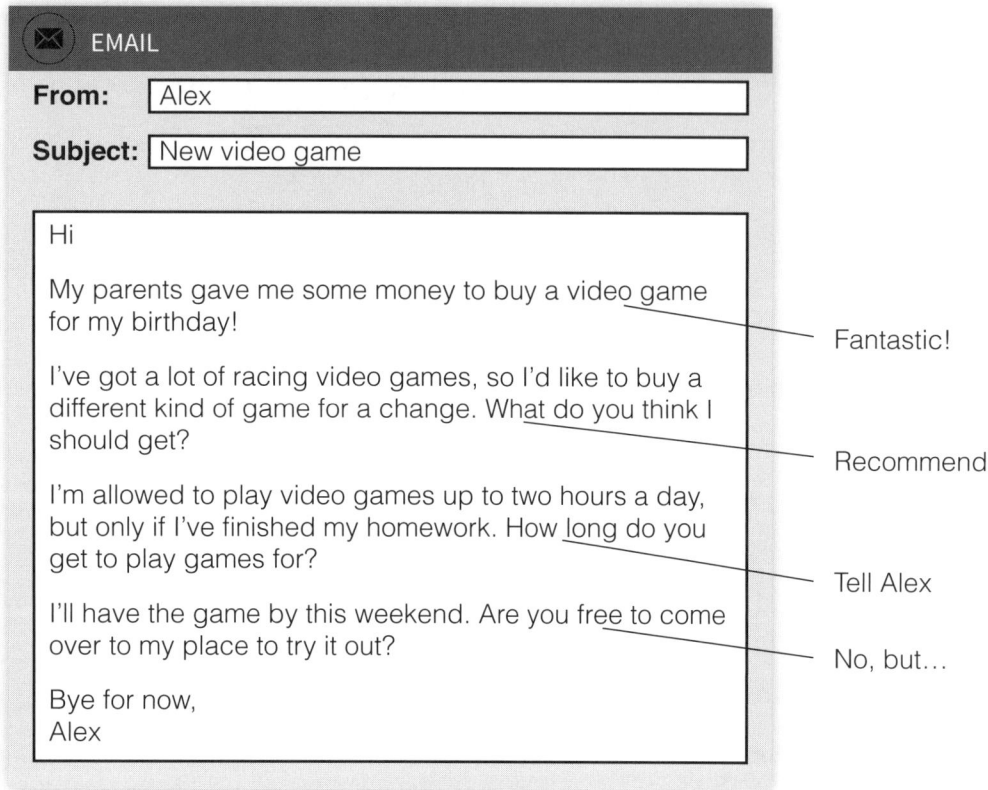

> **EMAIL**
>
> **From:** Alex
>
> **Subject:** New video game
>
> Hi
>
> My parents gave me some money to buy a video game for my birthday! — Fantastic!
>
> I've got a lot of racing video games, so I'd like to buy a different kind of game for a change. What do you think I should get? — Recommend
>
> I'm allowed to play video games up to two hours a day, but only if I've finished my homework. How long do you get to play games for? — Tell Alex
>
> I'll have the game by this weekend. Are you free to come over to my place to try it out? — No, but…
>
> Bye for now,
> Alex

Write your **email** to Alex using **all the notes**.

Choose **one** of these questions.
Write your answer in about **100 words** on the answer sheet.

....

Question 2

You see this notice in your school English-language magazine.

> **Articles wanted!**
>
> **SHOPPING**
> Write an article telling us whether
> you like shopping and where your
> family usually goes shopping.
> Does your family buy things online?
> Why or why not?
> The best articles answering
> these questions will be published
> next month.

Write your **article**.

Question 3

Your English teacher has asked you to write a story. Your story must begin
with this sentence:

Jasmin was at an exhibition when she noticed something unusual.

Write your **story**.

Questions 1–7

For each question, choose the correct answer.

1 Where is the boy's family going to eat?

A

B

C

2 Which lesson does the girl have next?

A

B

C

3 Where has the boy just been on holiday?

A

B

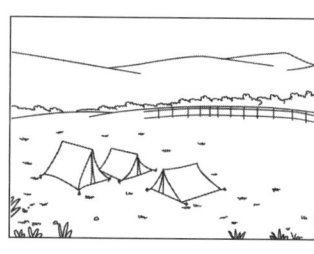

C

4 Which work experience would the girl like to try?

A

B

C

5 What did the boy leave at his friend's house?

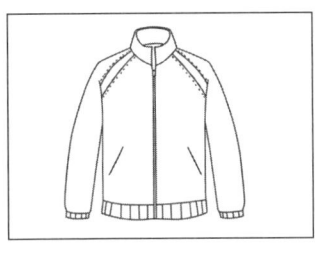

A

B

C

6 Which painting did the girl like best?

A

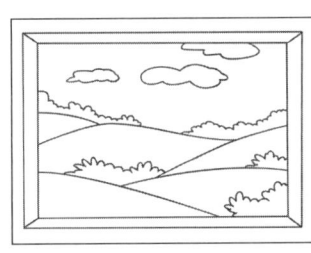

B

C

7 Where will the students' tour of the town end?

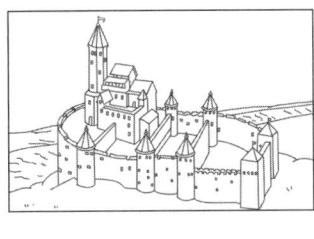

A

B

C

Questions 8–13

51   For each question, choose the correct answer.

8   You will hear a boy telling his friend about a snowboarding trip.
What problem did the boy have on the trip?

A   He damaged some equipment.

B   He injured himself.

C   He became ill.

9   You will hear two friends talking about the new library at their school.
The girl thinks that

A   the staff are helpful.

B   there should be more books.

C   it's a good place to do homework.

10   You will hear two friends talking about a new clothes shop.
They agree the shop would be better if

A   the assistants were more friendly.

B   there was more choice of clothes.

C   it was in the town centre.

11   You will hear two friends talking about a new classmate.
The boy thinks the new classmate

A   is very clever.

B   likes playing sport.

C   talks too much.

12   You will hear a girl talking about her big brother going away to college.
How does she feel about it?

A   pleased there's less noise

B   surprised that she's so sad

C   upset he's gone so far away

13   You will hear two friends talking about playing tennis.
The boy wants the girl to

A   practise with him regularly.

B   recommend a tennis coach.

C   teach him some new techniques.

🎧 **Questions 14–19**

52 For each question, write the correct answer in the gap.
Write **one** or **two words** or a **number** or a **date** or a **time**.

You will hear a teacher giving his students information about a school trip to a farm.

School trip to farm

Meeting place:	8 a.m. next to the **(14)** ....
Need to bring:	a **(15)** ....
Morning activity:	feeding the **(16)** ....
Afternoon activity:	**(17)** ....
Return to school at:	**(18)** ....
For more information:	**(19)** www. .... .farm.com

Questions 20–25

53 For each question, choose the correct answer.

···

You will hear an interview with a young hairdresser called Carlotta.

20 Carlotta first become interested in cutting people's hair when she saw
  A   a hairdressing magazine.
  B   a cartoon character doing it.
  C   a friend having it done.

21 The first hair that Carlotta cut belonged to
  A   her father.
  B   her sister.
  C   her mother.

22 At college, Carlotta's teachers said she should
  A   talk to customers more.
  B   spend more time planning.
  C   improve her cutting technique.

23 How did Carlotta feel during the Young Hairdresser competition?
  A   sure she would lose
  B   angry with the model
  C   confused by the rules

24 What does Carlotta say is the biggest benefit of working for a well-known company?
  A   meeting famous people
  B   making plenty of money
  C   gaining a variety of experience

25 What would Carlotta like to do next?
  A   open a hairdressing school
  B   create a range of beauty products
  C   start a business in another country

PART 1

(2–3 minutes)

Phase 1

Good morning / afternoon / evening

What's your name?

How old are you?

Where do you live?

Who do you live with?

Phase 2

(possible examiner questions)

What do you usually do in the morning before school?

Tell us about an interesting place you've visited.

What do you usually do during break times at school? (Why?)

What thing could you not live without? (Why?)

What did you do last weekend?

Which person you know makes you laugh the most? (Why are they so funny?)

What is your favourite time of year? (Why?)

Where did you go on your last holiday?

PART 2

(3–5 minutes)

Now I'd like each of you to talk on your own about something. I'm going to give each of you a photograph and I'd like you to talk about it.

A, here is your photograph. It shows **people enjoying music together**. (See page C5.)

B, you just listen.

A, please tell us what you can see in the photograph.

B, here is your photograph. It shows **someone taking a photo**. (See page C6.)

A, you just listen.

B, please tell us what you can see in the photograph.

PART 3

(4–5 minutes)

Now, in this part of the test you're going to talk about something together for about two minutes. I'm going to describe a situation to you.

A family want to do **an exciting activity** together that will be fun for everyone to do.

Here are some things they could do together. (See page C15.)

Talk together about the different **things** they could do together and say **which would be the most fun**.

All right? Now, talk together.

PART 4

(3–4 minutes)

What activity do you most enjoy doing with your family? (Why?)

Are there any exciting activities you'd like to try in the future? (Why?)

What do you think is the best time of year to go for a day out? (Why?)

Do you prefer to do activities with family or friends? (Why?)

Which do you think is more interesting: a day out in the city or a day out in the countryside? (Why?)

Questions 1–5

For each question, choose the correct answer.

1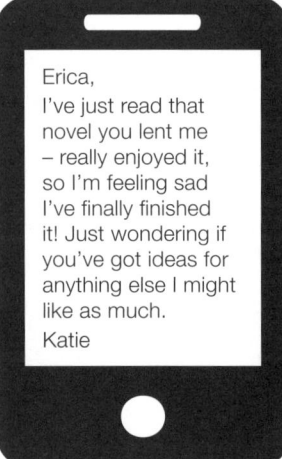

> Erica,
> I've just read that novel you lent me – really enjoyed it, so I'm feeling sad I've finally finished it! Just wondering if you've got ideas for anything else I might like as much.
> Katie

A Katie is upset that Erica hasn't returned the book she's borrowed.

B Katie disagrees with Erica about a book they've both just read.

C Katie wants some suggestions about what she could read next.

2

PLEASE DO NOT LEAVE BICYCLES HERE!

ENTRANCE IN USE NIGHT AND DAY

CYCLE PARK BEHIND BUILDING

A This entrance is only for use by cyclists who need to enter the building.

B You will prevent people entering and leaving if your bicycle is left here.

C There is somewhere you can leave your bicycle opposite this building.

3

New Message

From: Mr Davidson
To: Students

Thanks for attending the film show yesterday, and the director's interesting talk. The questions you asked him, and the lively discussion in class afterwards, showed you'd really thought about the film.

Why is Mr Davidson contacting students?

A to give his opinion of the film they watched together

B to suggest that they should spend another lesson talking about the film

C to congratulate them on the way they took part in a film event

4

UNDER-16s SAILING CLUB

Now taking new members

Limited spaces available

Club meets every Saturday – come along!

Fees: weekly or monthly

A Young people have the chance to learn some new watersports at this club.

B You don't need to pay for several sessions in advance at this club.

C To become a member at this club, apply by Saturday at the latest.

5

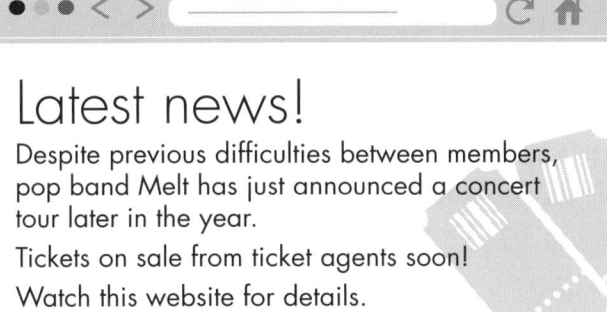

Latest news!

Despite previous difficulties between members, pop band Melt has just announced a concert tour later in the year.

Tickets on sale from ticket agents soon!

Watch this website for details.

A To attend a *Melt* tour concert, check the site regularly to find out more.

B You'll soon be able to buy tickets for *Melt*'s concerts on this website.

C *Melt* have just started touring again even though they've had problems in the band.

Questions 6–10

For each question, choose the correct answer.

The people below all want to find a department store to visit in their city.
On the opposite page there are descriptions of eight department stores.
Decide which department store would be the most suitable for the people below.

6  Jasmine would like to find a store where they can eat outside, and her dad wants somewhere known for its good-quality suits. They also want to buy a necklace for Jasmine's mum.

7 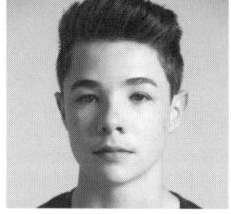 Peter wants to buy some special sweets for his grandma's birthday, and his older sister, Nell, wants to see the latest women's fashions. They also need to buy new tennis T-shirts, without spending a lot.

8  Maria wants a store selling clothes that use materials produced without damaging the environment. Her mum would like somewhere that has great customer service and is beautiful inside.

9  John enjoys cooking, and wants to buy some unusual ingredients. His parents like stores that have been in the same buildings since they were young, and that have great toys for John's young sister.

10  Samuel and Mark want to visit a store with a good selection of chess sets. They'd like to have some delicious ice creams and buy something made in the store to eat later.

Department stores

A ## Hallwick's

People often visit Hallwick's just for the displays of lights that make it so attractive to shop here. And it was the first to sell clothes made of pure, natural cotton, grown in conditions that avoid creating pollution. The assistants are polite and will help with any questions about goods.

B ## Crozier's

This store is in a beautiful new building. One floor is full of toys and board games like chess, and downstairs there's a huge variety of cakes, sweets and also fresh food that's perfect for making a meal! The roof garden is popular here in summer, and the friendly staff serve delicious lunches.

C ## Stafford's

This store is popular for its range of good-quality sportswear at very reasonable prices, which is hard to find elsewhere. And on the ground floor, you'll find displays of their famous handmade candies – great for celebrations! And Stafford's is always the first to offer new designs in men's and women's clothing, too!

D ## Barton's

Barton's has been here since it opened in 1930, and still has its huge glass door and beautiful windows. The first floor is fantastic for children, as it's packed with things to play with – at reasonable prices. And downstairs, you'll find a huge selection of amazing fresh food rarely found elsewhere.

E ## Gardener and Bell's

This store has been here since 1950, and is the place for cool clothes and jewellery, as it updates its items every few weeks – and many are made from environmentally-friendly materials. The sportswear section has clothes and equipment for almost any sport, although prices can be high.

F ## Davidson's

This traditional-looking store opened in 1860, and still offers high-class, fashionable goods at reasonable prices, with many made from natural materials. The men's clothes are particularly recommended, and there's also an area selling nothing but beautiful jewellery. And on fine days, try the rooftop restaurant – the food is fantastic.

G ## Ford and Madecroft's

The café here serves fantastic meals, but also has amazing chocolates and frozen desserts of all kind, and the bakers produce fantastic biscuits and cakes to take away. Upstairs, you'll find a display of toys and also a huge range of board games, together with instructions to help you play.

H ## Oldridge's

The customer service here is the best anywhere in the city, and staff will help you find what you're looking for, from jewellery to children's toys. And the café here, probably one of the most attractive you'll ever visit, serves the biggest ice creams anywhere, too – and the best cakes!

Questions 11–15

For each question, choose the correct answer.

Whale-watching trip
by Jack Madison, 15

A while ago, my friend Olivia was telling me about a whale-watching trip she'd been on, in Canada. I wanted to tell her I was about to do the same thing, off the north coast of the UK, where my grandparents live. Whales had recently appeared there again, and my grandparents were convinced we'd see some – so I was sure my trip would be as good as Olivia's! But then I saw some reviews of the trip my dad had booked for us, when no-one had seen *any* whales at all. So, in the end, I decided not to tell Olivia anything about my trip, in case it wasn't successful!

Anyway, Dad and I set off on our trip – which was Dad's idea – and it was fantastic! Travelling out to sea on the tour boat with our guide, we soon reached the spot where whales often appeared. Then we waited – and nothing happened. I was sure this wouldn't last, though. People kept calling out they'd seen one, which was exciting – but then it turned out they were wrong. Then finally I saw something move under the water – a minke whale! So I felt like a hero for the rest of the trip!

The whale was a wonderful sight, with its huge back not far from the boat. Our guide said it was around five tonnes in weight and around 10 metres long. Yet, despite its size, it swam alongside us at speed, and with little effort. We waited to see if more appeared, and some time later, we saw three more some distance away, that kept diving under the water and coming up again. Then just after I'd filmed them, they disappeared.

Although the water's less deep around the coast, larger whale species appear in the area with minke whales, feeding on fish. But minkes are curious creatures, so they're more likely to approach tourist boats – which was why we were successful! Then later, up on the cliffs, we looked out to sea, searching for signs of whales. Sometimes seabirds diving into the water means whales are around, as they're stealing the whales' meal. We were unlucky, sadly – but we'll be back!

11 Jack wasn't keen to mention his whale-watching trip to Olivia because

    A   he thought her trip sounded a lot more exciting.

    B   he'd read some negative reports about where he was going.

    C   he wasn't sure if his dad had definitely arranged it.

    D   he didn't know whether she was very interested in whales.

12 On board the whale-watching boat, Jack

    A   was proud to be the first person to see a whale.

    B   began to worry that they might all be disappointed.

    C   tried not to get excited when anyone saw something.

    D   was glad he'd persuaded his dad to come with him.

13 When Jack saw the minke whale, he was

    A   surprised at how close it came to the boat.

    B   amazed that it was so much bigger than he'd imagined.

    C   impressed that it moved through the water so easily.

    D   delighted to see it had arrived with several others.

14 Jack suggests minke whales appeared in the same area as the boat because

    A   they knew there were plenty of fish there.

    B   they were attracted by the arrival of the visitors.

    C   they didn't have to compete for food with seabirds.

    D   they preferred how deep the water was there.

15 What would Jack text to his grandparents about the whales?

A

> I'll send you my video of the group of whales – they only appeared briefly, so they weren't as interesting as the first one we saw.

B

> Dad said he'd really wanted to go to Canada to watch whales, like my friend Olivia – but now we're really happy we came here.

C

> I must take you up to the cliffs to look for whales – we've seen them every time we've been there, so far.

D

> You were so sure our whale-watching trip would be a success, while I still had doubts – but you were right.

Questions 16–20

Five sentences have been removed from the text below. For each question, choose the correct answer.
There are three extra sentences which you do not need to use.

What's the point in studying music?

Many children have music classes when they attend school. And it's thought that music can really help children with learning other subjects.

For example, one research project looked at what happened when a class of children were divided into groups and given a simple task to do, with one group listening to music while completing it, and the other completing the task in silence. **16** _____ The first group performed better than the second. So this seems to suggest that music can improve performance in certain areas.

So how exactly can you benefit from studying music? According to some studies, musical training can develop the part of your brain that's involved with language, so you can understand your own language better. **17** _____ And that's a very useful skill to have. What's more, young people who've studied music also seem to score more highly in other areas such as maths. **18** _____ For example, reading music includes learning about quarter and half notes, which are basically fractions, like in maths. And when you're learning about rhythm, you're counting the notes in a piece of music. So they do appear to be connected.

Music also lets you explore new ideas, think in a creative way, and gain in confidence. If you're learning the guitar, for example, it can be really exciting when you're able to start inventing your own pieces of music. And when you do that, you're practising your listening skills because you have to listen carefully to the music you're making. **19** _____ It's certainly essential when you join an orchestra, for example.

One of the biggest benefits, of course, is that listening to music helps you to be less stressed. **20** _____ That should always be in a relaxed atmosphere, though, to be effective. And who knows? Maybe your musical knowledge will open up a great career path for you in the future!

A   Students have also shared their own ideas about music.

B   And creating music can make you feel the same way.

C   So it could be that these school subjects are linked in some way.

D   These explain why music affects us in certain ways.

E   And there was a difference between the two.

F   It could also help with learning a second one.

G   But it isn't really what's happening.

H   This is particularly important when performing with other people.

Questions 21–26

For each question, choose the correct answer.

A brief history of apples

Do you always have a piece of fruit for your lunch? If you do, it's probably an apple! This is true particularly in places like western Europe, where apples have grown for hundreds of years. So it would be easy to (21) .... that's where they came from originally.

In fact, though, the fruit we know today has been on an extraordinary (22) .... over the centuries. Research suggests modern apples originally came all the way from Kazakhstan in Asia, and (23) .... up in Europe partly because of people carrying goods along the famous Silk Road, from western Europe all the way to China in the east. This helped to spread apples in both (24) .... People (25) .... down their apples after they'd finished eating them, and the seeds entered the ground and produced new types of apple trees. Farmers were then able to start developing a much (26) .... range of apples.

21	A consider	B wonder	C imagine	D expect
22	A distance	B travel	C course	D journey
23	A reached	B ended	C set	D kept
24	A routes	B ways	C directions	D paths
25	A threw	B dropped	C fell	D let
26	A longer	B deeper	C higher	D broader

Questions 27–32

For each question, write the correct word.
Write **one** word for each gap.

Learning to swim

by Sophie Webber

Last month, I did something amazing, which I'd almost begun to think wasn't possible. I actually swam one length of the swimming pool! I know it doesn't seem like **(27)** .... achievement, because swimming is something that everyone seems to learn really easily. But

there was just **(28)** .... way I could manage it. And it wasn't as if I hadn't tried. Apart **(29)** .... all the lessons I had at school, I also went swimming with Dad **(30)** .... week. But in **(31)** .... of all the practice I was getting, I still wasn't able to swim.

Then one day, when I thought Dad was holding me up in the water as usual, I suddenly realised – he wasn't! I was swimming on **(32)** .... own, without help! After that, I swam several lengths of the pool.

So if you're having trouble learning something, don't give up. It will definitely happen one day!

You **must** answer this question.

Write your answer in about **100 words** on the answer sheet.

Question 1

Read this email from your English teacher and the notes you have made.

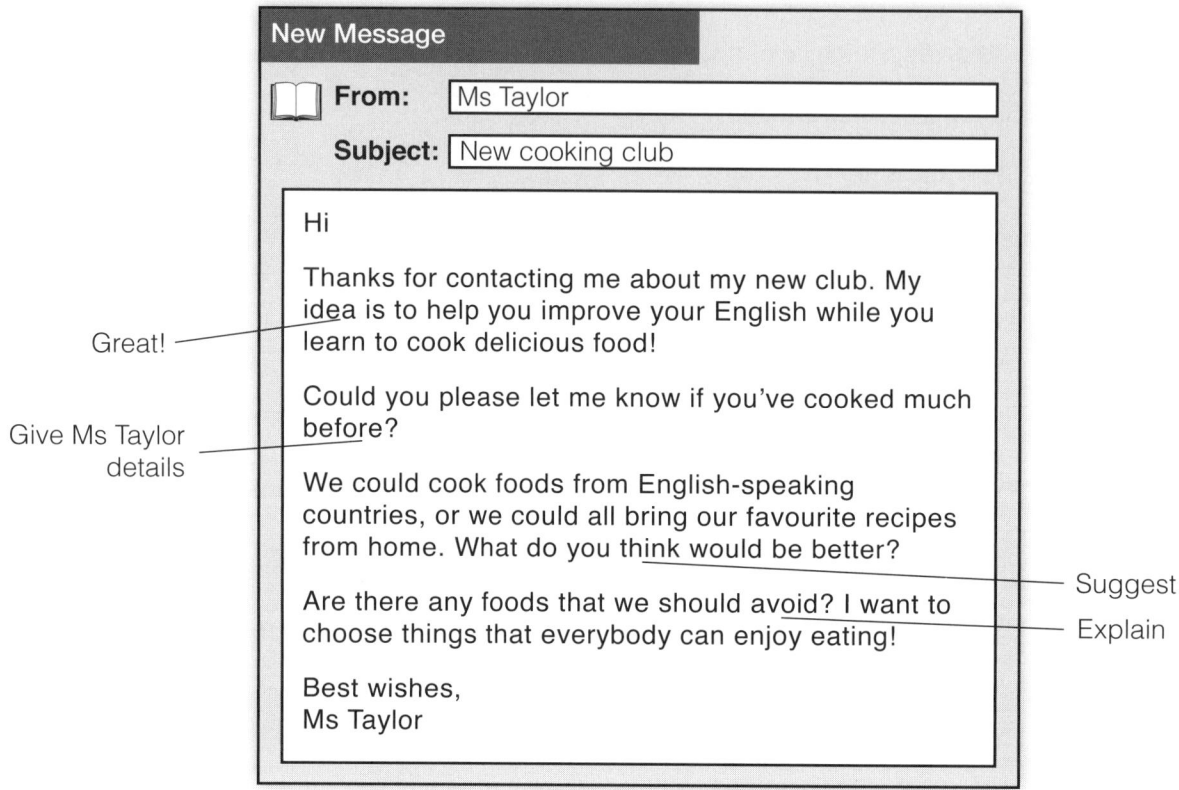

Great!

Give Ms Taylor details

New Message

From: Ms Taylor

Subject: New cooking club

Hi

Thanks for contacting me about my new club. My idea is to help you improve your English while you learn to cook delicious food!

Could you please let me know if you've cooked much before?

We could cook foods from English-speaking countries, or we could all bring our favourite recipes from home. What do you think would be better?

Are there any foods that we should avoid? I want to choose things that everybody can enjoy eating!

Best wishes,
Ms Taylor

Suggest

Explain

Write your **email** to Ms Taylor using **all the notes**.

Choose **one** of these questions.

Write your answer in about **100 words** on the answer sheet.

....

Question 2

You see this notice on an international English website for young people.

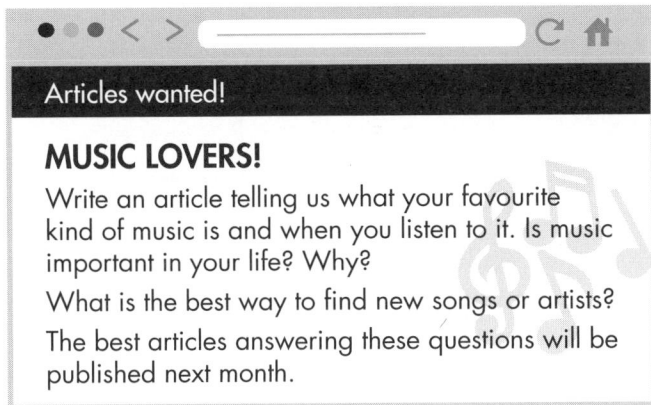

> **Articles wanted!**
>
> **MUSIC LOVERS!**
>
> Write an article telling us what your favourite kind of music is and when you listen to it. Is music important in your life? Why?
>
> What is the best way to find new songs or artists?
>
> The best articles answering these questions will be published next month.

Write your **article**.

Question 3

Your English teacher has asked you to write a story. Your story must begin with this sentence:

My family and I discovered a cave in the forest and we all decided to go in.

Write your **story**.

Questions 1–7

54   For each question, choose the correct answer.

1   How is the girl going to help her dad?

A   B   C

2   Which place would the boy most like to visit?

A   B   C

3   What's the girl learning to do?

A   B   C

4 What did the boy forget to buy?

A

B

C

5 Where did the girl leave her glasses?

A

B

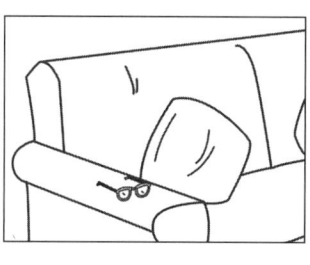

C

6 Why was the boy late for school?

A

B

C

7 What does Lisa's dad want her to do?

A

B

C

Questions 8–13

55   For each question, choose the correct answer.

....

8   You will hear two friends talking about working with other students in class.
The girl thinks that working with other students in class

A   is more useful for the lesson.

B   takes longer than working alone.

C   makes classes more fun.

9   You will hear two friends talking about a school trip to a museum.
The friends agree that

A   the exhibitions were all interesting.

B   there were nice things in the shop.

C   it was too large to see in one visit.

10   You will hear two friends talking about a football match.
The boy is feeling happy because

A   his team won.

B   he scored a goal.

C   his parents came to watch.

11   You will hear two friends talking about a poem they've read.
They think the poem would be better if

A   it was shorter.

B   it had a clearer meaning.

C   the sections were in a different order.

12   You will hear a boy asking a girl about an essay he has written.
The girl thinks the boy should

A   add more detail.

B   change the subject.

C   improve the style.

13   You will hear two friends talking about a video game.
Why is the boy talking to the girl about the video game?

A   to apologise

B   to make a request

C   to thank her

Questions 14–19

56   For each question, write the correct answer in the gap.
Write **one** or **two words** or a **number** or a **date** or a **time**.

....

You will hear a music teacher giving some information to students about Saturday music classes.

Saturday music classes

Classes available

- drums
- **(14)** ....
- guitar

On arrival

- go to the **(15)** .... to pick up your instrument

Cost

- **(16)** £ .... per class

End-of-term concert

- on **(17)** ....
- play alone or with the **(18)** ....
- friends and family welcome

For more information

- contact music teacher on **(19)** .... @school.net

Questions 20–25

57 For each question, choose the correct answer.

You will hear an interview with a young woman called Lin, who makes online videos about environmental issues.

20 How did Lin learn how to start putting videos online?

    A She did a short course.

    B She used information online.

    C She asked someone she knew.

21 Why did Lin choose to focus on the environment?

    A A teacher recommended this topic.

    B There were so few online videos about it.

    C She'd been interested in it for a long time.

22 How did Lin feel when her online videos first became successful?

    A surprised it happened so quickly

    B anxious about being seen by so many people

    C certain that she would get even more followers

23 Lin says that to become successful, people should put videos online

    A every day.

    B once a week.

    C once a month.

24 Lin's latest video is about

    A climate change.

    B public transport.

    C recycling.

25 Why does Lin think it's important for her to try new things?

    A to stop herself becoming bored

    B to learn more about the subject

    C to create discussion about the topic

PART 1

(2–3 minutes)

Phase 1

Good morning / afternoon / evening

What's your name?

How old are you?

Where do you live?

Who do you live with?

Phase 2

(possible examiner questions)

What are you going to do next weekend?

Where do you like to go with your friends? (Why?)

What do you usually do on your journey to school every day?

Which is your favourite meal of the day? (Why?)

Tell us about a relative you like spending time with.

Who is your favourite actor? (Why?)

What do you like about the area where you live? (Why?)

Tell us about the people you like visiting.

PART 2

(3–5 minutes)

Now I'd like each of you to talk on your own about something. I'm going to give each of you a photograph and I'd like you to talk about it.

A, here is your photograph. It shows **some friends meeting**. (See page C5.)

B, you just listen.

A, please tell us what you can see in the photograph.

B, here is your photograph. It shows **people doing something together in winter**. (See page C6.)

A, you just listen.

B, please tell us what you can see in the photograph.

PART 3

(4–5 minutes)

Now, in this part of the test you're going to talk about something together for about two minutes. I'm going to describe a situation to you.

A school would like to organise a talent show for students. The school wants to give **a prize** to the winner of the talent show.

Here are some prizes the school could give to the winner. (See page C16.)

Talk together about the different **prizes** the school could give to the winner of the talent show and say **which would be best**.

All right? Now, talk together.

PART 4

(3–4 minutes)

Do you ever watch talent shows on television? (Why? / Why not?)

Do you like taking part in competitions? (Why? / Why not?)

Is there anything that you are really good at? (What is it?)

If you could learn to do one new thing really well, what would you choose? (Why?)

Is it a good idea for schools to give prizes to students for doing well at school?

(Why? / Why not?)

Sample Answer Sheet for Reading

Cambridge Assessment
English

Candidate Name		Candidate Number	
Centre Name		Centre Number	
Examination Title		Examination Details	
Candidate Signature		Assessment Date	

Supervisor: If the candidate is ABSENT or has WITHDRAWN shade here ○

Preliminary for Schools Reading Candidate Answer Sheet

Instructions
Use a PENCIL (B or HB)
Rub out any answer you want to change with an eraser.

For Parts 1, 2, 3, 4 and 5:
Mark ONE letter for each answer.
For example: If you think A is the right answer to the question, mark your answer sheet like this:

0 A● B○ C○

Part 1

	A	B	C
1	○	○	○
2	○	○	○
3	○	○	○
4	○	○	○
5	○	○	○

Part 2

	A	B	C	D	E	F	G	H
6	○	○	○	○	○	○	○	○
7	○	○	○	○	○	○	○	○
8	○	○	○	○	○	○	○	○
9	○	○	○	○	○	○	○	○
10	○	○	○	○	○	○	○	○

Part 3

	A	B	C	D
11	○	○	○	○
12	○	○	○	○
13	○	○	○	○
14	○	○	○	○
15	○	○	○	○

Part 4

	A	B	C	D	E	F	G	H
16	○	○	○	○	○	○	○	○
17	○	○	○	○	○	○	○	○
18	○	○	○	○	○	○	○	○
19	○	○	○	○	○	○	○	○
20	○	○	○	○	○	○	○	○

Part 5

	A	B	C	D
21	○	○	○	○
22	○	○	○	○
23	○	○	○	○
24	○	○	○	○
25	○	○	○	○
26	○	○	○	○

Continues over ➡

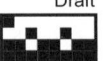

Sample Answer Sheet for Reading

Draft

For Part 6:
Write your answers clearly in the spaces next to the numbers (27 to 32) like this:

0 | E N G L I S H

Write your answers in CAPITAL LETTERS.

Part 6		Do not write below here
27		27 1 ○ 0 ○
28		28 1 ○ 0 ○
29		29 1 ○ 0 ○
30		30 1 ○ 0 ○
31		31 1 ○ 0 ○
32		32 1 ○ 0 ○

Draft

Sample Answer Sheet for Writing

You must write within the grey lines.

Write your answer for Part 1 below. Do not write on the barcodes.

Question 1

This section for use by Examiner only:

C	CA	O	L

Sample Answer Sheet for Writing

You must write within the grey lines.

Answer only one of the two questions for Part 2.
Tick the box to show which question you have answered.
Write your answer below. Do not write on the barcodes.

Part 2	Question 2		Question 3	

This section for use by Examiner only:

C	CA	O	L

* 0010446611103 *

Sample Answer Sheet for Listening

Cambridge Assessment English

Candidate Name		**Candidate Number**	
Centre Name		**Centre Number**	
Examination Title		**Examination Details**	
Candidate Signature		**Assessment Date**	

Supervisor: If the candidate is ABSENT or has WITHDRAWN shade here ○

Preliminary for Schools Listening Candidate Answer Sheet

Instructions

Use a PENCIL (B or HB). Rub out any answer you want to change with an eraser.

For Parts 1, 2 and 4:
Mark one letter for each answer. For example: If you think **A** is the right answer to the question, mark your answer sheet like this:

For Part 3:
Write your answers clearly in the spaces next to the numbers (14 to 19) like this:

Write your answers in CAPITAL LETTERS.

Part 1

	A	B	C
1	○	○	○
2	○	○	○
3	○	○	○
4	○	○	○
5	○	○	○
6	○	○	○
7	○	○	○

Part 2

	A	B	C
8	○	○	○
9	○	○	○
10	○	○	○
11	○	○	○
12	○	○	○
13	○	○	○

Part 3

		Do not write below here
14		14 1 ○ 0 ○
15		15 1 ○ 0 ○
16		16 1 ○ 0 ○
17		17 1 ○ 0 ○
18		18 1 ○ 0 ○
19		19 1 ○ 0 ○

Part 4

	A	B	C
20	○	○	○
21	○	○	○
22	○	○	○
23	○	○	○
24	○	○	○
25	○	○	○

Draft

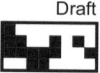

Acknowledgements

Our highly experienced team of Trainer writers, in collaboration with Cambridge Assessment English reviewers, have worked together to bring you *Preliminary for Schools Trainer 1*. We would like to thank Judy Alden (writer and reviewer), Sarah Curtis (writer), Sue Elliott (writer), Mark Little (writer), Peter May (writer), Claire Wijayatilake (writer), Sarah Dymond (reviewer) and Helen Tiliouine (reviewer) for their work on the material.

Author

The authors and publishers acknowledge the following sources of copyright material and are grateful for the permissions granted. While every effort has been made, it has not always been possible to identify the sources of all the material used, or to trace all copyright holders. If any omissions are brought to our notice, we will be happy to include the appropriate acknowledgements on reprinting and in the next update to the digital edition, as applicable.

Photographs

The following photographs are sourced from Getty Images:

T1: Cultura RM Exclusive/Nancy Honey; Westend61; Compassionate Eye Foundation/Chris Windsor/DigitalVision; Image Source; Plume Creative/DigitalVision; Justin Lambert/DigitalVision; Marc Dozier/Corbis Documentary; John Elk/Lonely Planet Images; Cultura RM Exclusive/ Stuart Westmorland; De Agostini/G. Dagli Orti/De Agostini Picture Library; Hero Images; Wavebreakmedia/iStock/Getty Images Plus; Robert Warren/The Image Bank; Eric Audras/ONOKY; **T2:** Jack Hollingsworth/Blend Images; jr_images/iStock/Getty Images Plus; drbimages/E+; fabbfoto/Moment; Plume Creative/DigitalVision; Tony Anderson/Taxi; Steve Mason/Photodisc; Loop Images/Gordon Scammell/Passage; All copyrights reserved by Harris Hui/Moment Open; aquasolid/iStock/Getty Images Plus; Norbert Eisele-Hein/LOOK-foto; webphotographeer/E+; Blend Images - JGI/Jamie Grill/Brand X Pictures; Eva-Katalin/E+; **T3:** cglade/iStock/Getty Images Plus; LordRunar/E+; Audrey Saracco/EyeEm; kate_sept2004/E+; Ron Levine/The Image Bank; Benjamin Knofe/EyeEm; CTRPhotos/iStock Editorial/Getty Images Plus; benjaminjk/iStock/ Getty Images Plus; kali9/E+; **T4:** Marcus Lindstrom/E+; Westend61; Siri Stafford/The Image Bank; Youngoldman/iStock/Getty Images Plus; Image Source/DigitalVision; Dennis Welsh/The Image Bank; Linda Thompson/Moment; JGI/Jamie Grill/Blend Images; filadendron/E+; **T5:** Johner Images; Jupiterimages/Photolibrary; Emelyn Cabacungan Wong/EyeEm; fstop123/iStock/ Getty Images Plus; Radius Images; Blend Images - John Lund/Marc Romanelli/Brand X Pictures; Nikada/E+; Westend61; Caiaimage/Sam Edwards; **T6:** Eric Lafforgue/Art in All of Us/Corbis News; Westend61; Vinit Deekhanu/EyeEm; Ron Levine/Photographer's Choice; Michael Blann/ DigitalVision; Yaorusheng/Moment; Anna Kucherova/iStock/Getty Images Plus; ArtBoyMB/E+; **End Matter:** svetikd/E+; Kevin Dodge/Blend Images; Steve Debenport/E+; Fuse/Corbis; Laszlo Podor/Moment; Ryan McVay/DigitalVision; Catherine Delahaye/DigitalVision; Hill Street Studios/ Blend Images; Yuri_Arcurs/E+; Kathrin Ziegler/Taxi; Hero Images; Westend61; Steve Debenport/ E+; Jeffrey Greenberg/Universal Images Group; Jim Arbogast/DigitalVision; Klaus Vedfelt/ DigitalVision; Eva-Katalin/E+; Blend Images - JGI/Jamie Grill/ Brand X Pictures; Robert Warren/ The Image Bank.

The following image is sourced from another library:

T6: Sorin Papuc/Alamy Stock Photo/Alamy.

Commissioned photography by: Trevor Clifford Photography.

Illustrations by QBS Learning.

Audio recordings by DN and AE Strauss Ltd. Engineer: Neil Rogers; Editor: James Miller; Producer; Dan Strauss. Recorded at Half Ton Studios, Cambridge.

Notes

Notes

Notes

Notes

Notes

Candidate A

Candidate A

Candidate B

Candidate B

Candidate A

Candidate A

Candidate B

Candidate B

Candidate A

Candidate A

Candidate B

Candidate B

Candidate C

Candidate C

Candidate C

Candidate C

Candidate C

Candidate C

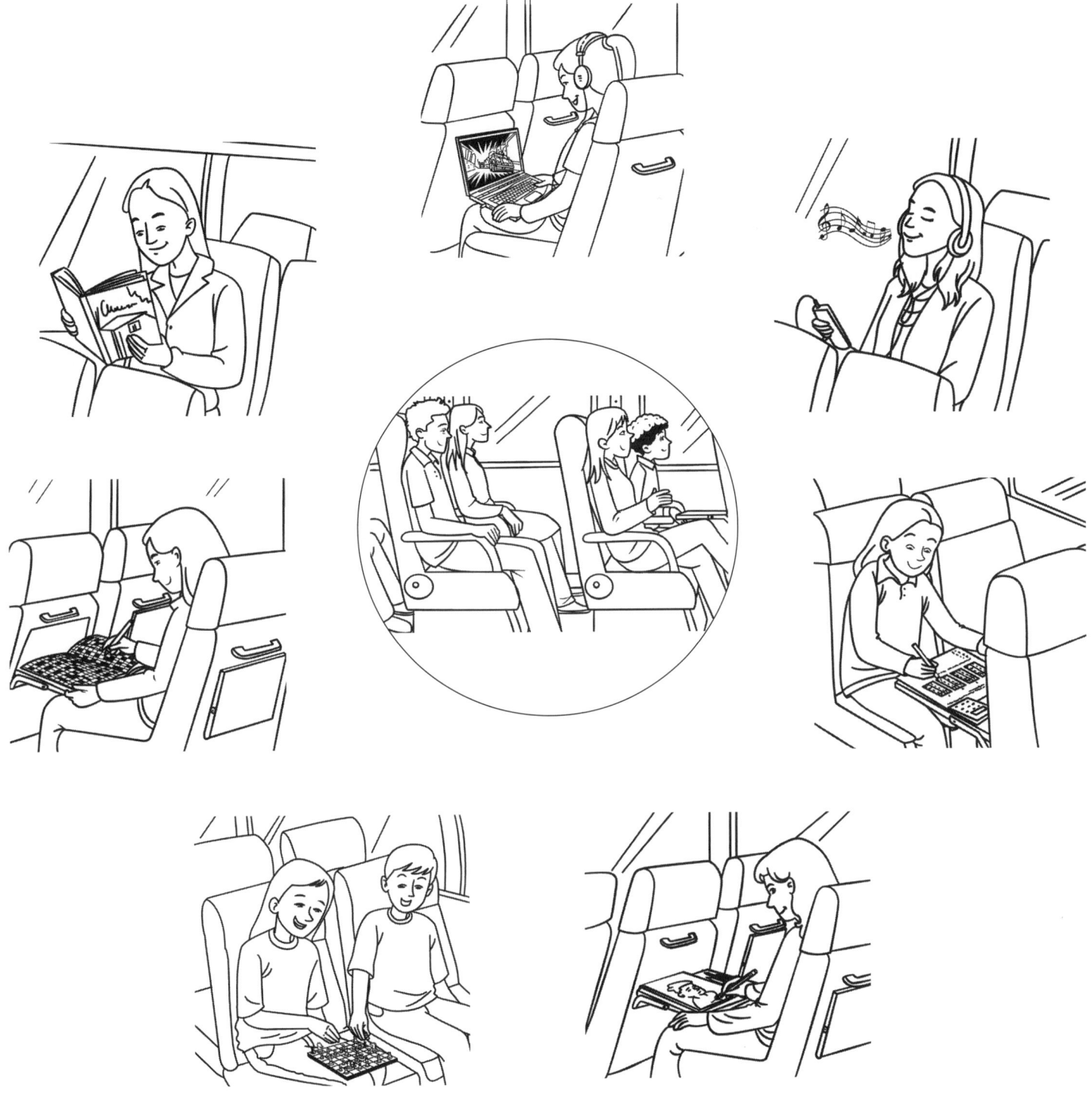

Space

Class Trip

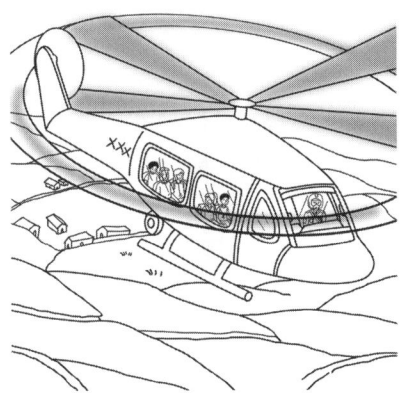

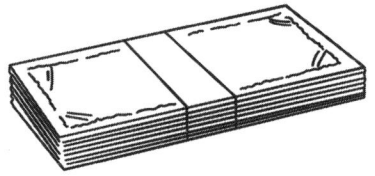